SPEAK EASY

CONNECT WITH EVERY CONVERSATION

LOU DIAMOND

PAGE TWO

Cataloguing in publication information is available from
Library and Archives Canada.
ISBN 978-1-77458-185-8 (paperback)
ISBN 978-1-77458-186-5 (ebook)
ISBN 978-1-77458-272-5 (audiobook)

Page Two
pagetwo.com

Edited by Amanda Lewis
Copyedited by Rachel Ironstone
Cover design by Cameron McKague
Interior design by Jennifer Lum
Printed and bound in Canada by Friesens
Distributed in Canada by Raincoast Books
Distributed in the US and internationally by Macmillan

22 23 24 25 26   5 4 3 2 1

ThriveLouD.com

J,
My love, my life
and the easiest person to speak to.

Contents

INTRO

---

*"One good conversation can
shift the direction of change forever."*

LINDA LAM

AFTER TAKING OVER a dozen looks at herself in the hotel room's mirror, Sara glanced at her watch and realized she was going to be late.

She cursed a few times and grabbed her iPhone, her key card and her event conference badge with its blue-ribbon attachment that read "SPEAKER."

She dashed down the long corridor, jumped into the elevator, repeatedly pressed the "CASINO / LOBBY" button until the doors shut, and prayed she'd have an express ride.

The elevator arrived after no stops, and Sara dashed through the lobby in her steam-pressed dress and five-inch heels. She had the length of five football fields to cover to get to the conference center of the Aria Resort & Casino in Las Vegas.

"Excuse me, which way to the main ballroom?" she hurriedly asked a random group of lanyard-wearing conference attendees.

After some general uncertainty and a noncommittal "down that corridor?" directive, Sara again checked her watch and saw she'd be cutting it close but was going to be okay after all.

Upon reaching the main hall entrance, she met eyes with the event producer, who was equally panicked about Sara's arrival time.

The producer hurriedly guided her toward a back pathway adjacent to the main ballroom and began weaving the wires and cords of a lavalier microphone down her back and into an inconspicuous location beneath her dress that would be out of view of the audience.

Standing backstage, Sara had a few minutes before she was to deliver her speech as the featured keynote speaker of a multiday conference.

She was pumped and extremely nervous, as this would be the largest audience she had ever addressed.

The bustling sound of over four thousand people finding their seats was now evident to Sara. She heard the event's emcee letting everyone know all about the next speaker.

Sara was tempted to peek through the side curtain to view the audience but thought better of it and began her "pregame" routine.

She closed her eyes, took a few slow deep breaths and appreciated the moment.

While she tried to deploy her recently discovered meditation exercises, she had too many thoughts racing and wasn't able to settle her mind.

In particular, one thought repeated: "How did I get here?"

Instead of dismissing it, she decided to retrace the memories of what had brought her to this moment, as a way to relax herself before going onstage.

She remembered her excitement to fly to Las Vegas in an upgraded business class seat. Before that, she neatly packed her Away branded carry-on bag, her onstage outfit placed inside without a crease.

Prior to that were numerous coordination efforts with the event team to prep for her presentation. Before that were many rehearsals of her speech and video conference calls with the event-planning team to craft a message that would connect to this year's theme.

Months before, she delivered a final pitch presentation to the event-planning committee tasked with selecting their featured speaker.

Even further back in time, she received an email from that very same committee asking her to submit a proposal to speak at this conference.

And weeks before that email was a phone call. One simple call with the head of sales for one of the largest companies in North America, who wanted to learn more about Sara.

That was it. Sara recognized that was where it all began: with just one conversation.

One conversation that established a connection.

One conversation that began a relationship.

One conversation that sparked an idea.

One conversation that opened the door for Sara to share her brilliance.

One conversation that created the possibility that Sara would be able to help this executive's sales team with her message.

One conversation that stimulated the idea that Sara could be a fantastic speaker to keynote the company's upcoming global conference.

Remembering that initial conversation and the connection she made, Sara smiled, took a breath and walked onto the stage to thunderous applause.

One Great Conversation

Each one of us, in our own way, strives to have moments like Sara did on her big day.

We all remember and rejoice in the milestones and memories that greatly impact our lives.

But we can all feel so frazzled and swept up in the moment that we forget how we arrived here.

Sara was able to retrace her long journey to the big stage, this pivotal moment in her career, to one great conversation.

Was she right?

When you think about every business relationship you have made in your life, every friendship, all of the meaningful connections you have created...

They all began with an engaging *conversation* where you *connected* with someone or some group of people.

Great conversations are at the heart of the great connections in our lives.

Conversations have the power to inspire, motivate, engage and educate us.

Conversations start the engine so we can drive toward the connections we desire to make.

And because of their strength and value, we plan our days around them. We seek out new ways to have better, deeper, more authentic conversations that will enrich our lives.

I think Sara was on to something.

But I also know that not *every* conversation is a *great* conversation.

Many times, we fail to make a strong connection when speaking with another.

That promising lead turns out to be a bust.

That first date we were excited about doesn't lead to a second.

That hard conversation we led doesn't result in change for either party.

Nor did that sales pitch we gave land the prospective client.

Not all conversations lead to a great result, a triumph or a win.

But what if they could?

What if you knew the key elements that have the potential to make every conversation great?

What if you knew the steps to "set up" each conversation to increase the likelihood that you connect, engage and win?

What if you had a road map to guide each of your good conversations into great ones?

Speak Easy

During the Prohibition era, underground and illegal bars called speakeasies emerged. They received their name from police officers who had trouble locating the bars because patrons tended to speak quietly, at the bartenders' request, while inside the hidden drinking spots.

Many of these venues were secret, often the backrooms of legitimate storefronts, requiring secret passwords or special knocks to be allowed inside.

Today, you have been granted entry into a very special speakeasy.

On tap are not the usual ale house lagers or bathtub gins. Nor will I, as your guide and de facto mixologist, serve up anything illegal or of ill-repute.

Rather, you will be given access to some of the best kept secrets of some of the world's elite interviewers and conversationalists.

You have a front-row seat to a storyteller and professional speaker, who has rehearsed, presented and studied how content can connect and engage audiences.

You have tapped the ear of a podcaster who has listened, conducted, reviewed, dissected, analyzed, edited and broken down thousands of interviews and great conversations.

You have exclusive access to a sales professional and trainer, who has captured proven strategies, tactics and lessons and distilled them into this simple, easy-to-understand book.

In this *Speak Easy*, you will learn the skills and develop the tools you need to increase the likelihood that more of your conversations lead to great connections.

Speak Easy will address the mindset you should strive to be in before, during and after you have a conversation, as well as how to prepare, maximize and continue a great conversation.

Speak Easy will show you how to utilize a conversation to connect with prospects; engage with partners, clients and colleagues; and win in business and in life.

CONNECT, ENGAGE & WIN

At the end of each chapter is a section titled "Connect, Engage & Win" in which you will find tips, techniques and best practices utilized by some of the world's greatest communicators and leaders.

The suggestions in these sections are specifically geared toward connecting with business prospects and targets. You will receive tips for engaging your audience to win the sales, deals and relationships you need to get your business to thrive.

Think of *Speak Easy* as your playbook to tap into the unlimited potential that lies in every conversation.

Your seat at the bar is waiting for you. Come on in, be cool and learn something new.

1

CONVERSATIONS MATTER

"Can we talk?"

JOAN RIVERS

WELCOME!
I'm so glad you decided to visit this fine establishment. I want you to have a very relaxed and enjoyable time as you take in all that I have to offer.

While I begin to pull together a few creative concoctions for you, I think it'll help if I provide you with a little background as to what this specific Speak Easy *is all about.*

What Counts as Conversation?

We are enamored with conversations.

We enjoy listening to conversations we aren't even a part of, eavesdropping on the conversations of others!

We react, laugh, cry when hearing conversations that resonate with us.

We tune in to prime-time television to watch people have conversations.

We scour the internet and watch videos of interviews and conversations.

We listen to hundreds, if not thousands, of podcast interviews.

We are consistently drawn into conversations from every direction.

On any given day, you have numerous interactions and conversations. Your partner and kids in the morning, your driver or train conductor, your barista, your colleagues at the office.

The Courage Beer Conversations survey conducted in Britain in 2010 showed that the average person has more than twenty-five conversations each day.

When we traditionally think about the word "conversation," we think of two people speaking to one another. But here's how the dictionary defines it (emphasis mine):

> a talk between *two or more people* in which thoughts, feelings, and ideas are expressed, questions are asked and answered, or news and information is exchanged.

So, a conversation can take place among a group of people, like within a small team gathering or even a group presentation.

One could even go so far as saying that a conversation is taking place when someone is speaking to a large audience and interacting with them, like a keynote speaker presenting to several hundred or thousand attendees. Even a virtual presentation, in which a presenter delivers a message digitally and interactively, could be considered a conversation.

The lessons you'll take in here address all of these types of conversations that we encounter in our personal and professional lives.

We Need Conversations

Because of how commonplace conversations are, I suspect that most people take for granted the ones they have each day. However, since conversations are one of the means through which we can learn, develop and be informed, they are an essential part of our daily survival.

Simply put, we need conversations to live!

Conversations are key to language development and the exchange of thoughts and ideas. People learn empathy by hearing each other's thoughts while observing facial and body expressions that show emotions.

In her book *Reclaiming Conversation: The Power of Talk in a Digital Age*, Sherry Turkle writes,

Face-to-face conversation is the most human and humanizing thing we do. Fully present to one another, we learn to listen. It is where we develop the capacity for empathy. It's where we experience the joy of being heard and of being understood. Conversation advances self-reflection, the conversations with ourselves that are the cornerstone of early development and continue throughout life.

Plus, it turns out we equally desire to have conversations as part of our social fabric.

Harvard psychology professor Daniel Gilbert co-authored a study published in the *Proceedings of the National Academy of Sciences*. Within the study's conclusions, Gilbert stated, "Humans are the most social animal on the planet and conversation is the bread and butter of social life. We may not live by bread alone, but we die without it."

In summary, we are social beings, and we truly *need* to have conversations to thrive.

We Love Conversations

Conversations are like a cool, refreshing beverage that quenches our thirst to connect with others.

And the enlightenment, sense of empathy and appreciation that we derive from being involved in a conversation make us want to continue to have more of them.

Here's the cool thing about conversations: we don't even need to be the one who's having a conversation in order to enjoy it.

Conversations are one of the most popular forms of entertainment across multiple mediums.

Since the early days of radio and television, conversations have been traveling across the airwaves via interview programs, talk shows and informative broadcasts.

Since the 1960s, late-night talk show television has been recognized as the apex of weeknight programming. Each evening after the local news, millions have tuned in over the years to watch talk show legends—Jack Paar, Johnny Carson, Joan Rivers, David Letterman, Jay Leno, Conan O'Brien, Jimmy Kimmel, Jimmy Fallon, Jon Stewart and Stephen Colbert, to name a few— deliver their opening monologues and comic bits, all in a lead-up to the evening's main attraction: an interview with a celebrity guest.

For most of the television-watching world, these late-night conversations were the last bit of entertainment people needed to see before shutting their eyes.

The interview format is also popular at other times during the broadcast day.

National morning news programs, local news shows, mid-morning and mid-afternoon talk shows all feature conversations that millions of viewers enjoy while earning high ratings for the networks. Oprah Winfrey ruled the after-school–pre-dinner time slot for decades.

Comedian Joan Rivers even used the platform of having a conversation as her signature opening when she asked a live audience, "Can we talk?" While she was the only one speaking, her delivery suggested she was having a fun, light-hearted conversation with each individual member of the audience.

Joan made this "conversation" the act itself.

The emergence and subsequent explosive growth of the internet has only amplified and accelerated the amount of conversational content we consume.

If you're like me, you're probably *not* staying up every evening to watch those late-night talk show interview segments. More than likely, you are probably watching the video feeds from the show the following morning.

Millions more are also watching these clips on YouTube and then sharing them across social media. These exchanges are also conversations. While we're watching after the fact, we continue the conversation through social channels.

Let's Take a Look behind the Bar

Our desire to absorb more conversations continues to grow, as seen through the exponential growth of podcasting.

For those unfamiliar, a podcast is a digital audio or video file or recording, usually part of a themed series, that can be downloaded from a website to a media player or computer.

According to Edison Research and Triton Digital's annual study, *The Infinite Dial*, at the beginning of 2020 in the United States, there were more than 850,000 podcasts. That number more than doubled to over two million programs by April 2021, with over 48 million episodes.

The most popular format of podcast programming, making up over 85 percent of all podcasts, is interview-based or multi-host. Another term for this format is "recorded conversations."

The following two charts highlight the ever-growing appetite for podcasts and conversations as content.

The first highlights the overall growth of podcast listeners since 2014 in the United States alone. The expectation is the current listenership will double by 2023.

The second chart shows the amount of time per week that we spend listening to podcasts.

In short, while we don't know exactly how many Americans are listening to podcasts, what we do know is that listenership is increasing.

We haven't reduced our love of listening to others' conversations, we've just changed the medium by which we do so.

Podcast Audience Growth Rate, 2020

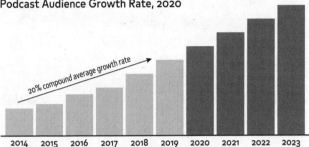

Source: Nielsen Podcast Listener Buying Power Database

Average Time Spent Listening to Podcasts

Ages 12+ in US and listened to podcast in last week
Hours:Minutes in Last Week

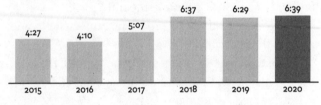

Source: *The Infinite Dial*

The Interview Format

Our need for conversations, driven by well-spoken, engaging hosts, explains why we continue to watch and listen to conversations as entertainment.

The actual structure and format of an interview-type conversation does not differ too much from show to show, whether late-night or podcast.

And just like you wouldn't improvise when making an Old Fashioned, why mess with this winning formula?

Run of Show

Long-running radio, television and podcast programs adhere to a well-structured and familiar "run of show."

A run of show is used for almost every event, live program or recorded production. It is a way of simplifying and distilling information that is essential to running a live show from beginning to end.

At its core, the running of show is an actual document that lays out the timing, program and content for each moment of an event. This format helps to keep shows of any kind or any scale running smoothly.

And a smooth-running program connects with and engages the audience.

In hosting my own podcast show, *Thrive LOUD*, I follow a run of show to make sure the podcast program is well structured and remains on track.

The layout and format of the run of show for the program is a helpful guide and structure for a conversation as well.

The flow from "intro" to "outro" encompasses a logical progression that is designed to connect with and engage the participants having the conversation as well as anyone listening to it.

When a conversation follows the run of show flow, there is a much higher likelihood that there will be a meaningful connection and stronger engagement.

Let me top off that drink, and let's run through it together. The run of show flow is not only a useful guide to navigate conversations, it also sets the framework for the easy-to-follow structure of *Speak Easy*.

Speak Easy: The Show Flow

This proven run of show flow is a helpful road map to guide you with every conversation.

Now I want to reiterate that your conversations need not stick *exactly* to the run of show flow.

Part of the art, magic and wonder of every conversation is its extemporaneous nature. And the beauty and purpose of having a conversation is to make a connection to another.

But while the road from which a conversation begins and ends isn't cemented in stone, having a smooth road with a few guard rails can help keep things on track.

Just as it has done time and time again for many successful interview-based programs, the run of show flow will keep you on the path toward having more great conversations.

But before we get into the run of show flow we throw around here at the *Speak Easy*, the next chapter will go over what elements of a conversation make it engaging in the first place.

CONNECT, ENGAGE & WIN

Too often throughout my career I have witnessed sales professionals, team leaders and CEOs approach their sales and client meetings as a business *presentation*.

Hours upon hours would be spent perfecting slide decks. Detailed scripts were created to address what needed to be said for each specific slide at the exact moment it would be onscreen in the meeting.

But these over-staged performances designed to sway or convince prospects are rarely effective.

Why? Because by delivering a presentation you are *telling* your targets what *you* think they want versus *asking* them what *they* really need.

By approaching a meeting with the mindset that you need to present who you are and tell them what you do, you're more focused on delivering a performance than establishing a connection and engaging with them.

Rather than approaching a business meeting as a dog and pony show, try to engage in a conversation.

Asking questions, viewing reactions and listening to what your prospects have to say will create a more stimulating environment for your meeting. It also will create a more engaging, vibrant environment that is way more enjoyable than having to watch the uninviting and uneventful "PowerPoint march of death."

Remember that we all love and need more conversations in our lives.

Ditch the slides and the scripts. Take the initiative and have a conversation in all your business meetings.

2

WHAT MAKES A CONVERSATION ENGAGING?

"Conversation may be compared to a lyre with seven chords—philosophy, art, poetry, politics, love, scandal, and the weather."

ANNA JAMESON

CONVERSATIONS ARE A form of content.

The combined words, sentences, questions, answers, reactions and back-and-forth discussion is content that we can absorb.

And while not all content is entertaining to everyone, there are certain elements in the form of a conversation that can make it more engaging than others.

Engaging Conversations = Great Content
and
Engaging Content = Great Conversations

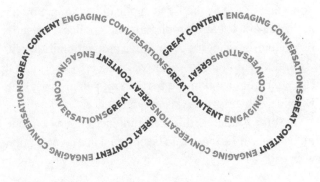

In my role as a professional speaker, I've spent my career understanding and experimenting with what type of content can engage an audience.

And as a podcaster, I've learned what makes a conversation interesting and engaging to a listening audience.

It turns out they are composed of the same familiar elements, which I call "The Seven Cs of Engagement." In the spirit of this seaworthy mnenomic, I recommend a maritime martini, foghorn or a salty dog to sip from as I walk you through it.

Set Sail! The Seven Cs of Engagement

Having a high-level understanding of what you need to engage your audience will help you think about what you can inject into your conversations.

Many of them are probably very familiar to you, and, funnily enough, they all start with the letter C. Also, thankfully, there are seven, as "The Six Cs" just doesn't have the same ring to it.

As you read through, you'll begin to better understand how each of the Seven Cs is applicable to engaging an audience at a theatre production, in a podcast episode, on a television show or even with a motivational speech.

And as you think of a *conversation as content*, you'll start to recognize that the participant you are speaking with in a conversation . . . is *your* audience.

In some instances, this is an audience of one—but one individual who is looking to be engaged in a conversation with you.

A few thoughts on the Seven Cs before we run through them.

- Not every conversation is going to have all seven of the Cs within it. Look for the Cs, but don't force them.

- I am completely aware that you will not remember what each of the Seven Cs is. That's what this book is for! Refer to *Speak Easy* when you need a memory aid.

- Focus on how each of the Seven Cs can help *your* conversation be more engaging with *your* audience.

- The more you can incorporate the Seven Cs, the greater the likelihood you'll elevate your conversations. Ever have a great cab ride or an enjoyable flight? Chances are a good conversation was part of it.

Content

The first C in engaging your audience is content.

More specifically, it is *familiar content*.

We like to speak about things that we are familiar with.

We are more likely to choose to engage in a conversation if the topic or material is something we are comfortable with and understand.

Whether we're an active participant in the conversation or we are taking in a conversation from afar with our eyes and ears, we prefer familiar topics.

If we are familiar with the topic or the person who is speaking, we will be more engaged than we would be with a concept we don't know or an individual we are unfamiliar with.

This is why so many people are intrigued by celebrities that appear on talk shows. We are familiar with who they are so we are drawn in to learn more about them. We will find any conversation engaging if there is a famous person involved, whether we like them or not.

This is the reason why TV talk show interviews are so similar—bring on that famous person and we'll be entertained and engaged just by hearing them speak to the host.

When we are familiar with the topic, we probably have preformed opinions and an endless appetite to hear more.

Makes sense, right? Think of a topic you have a bottomless interest in. Now imagine your favorite celebrity is about to speak about it. Leaned in a little closer, did you?

Context

Whereas *content* is the material that you can share with your audience, *context* is the setting or circumstance in which a person connects with your content. Context gives content meaning.

Content unto itself can be pretty straightforward and filled with tremendous value. However, it becomes even more engaging when you can contextualize that content in a familiar setting.

The power of providing an example that your audience can relate to amplifies the message.

Billionaire investor Warren Buffett has this saying: "Hire well, manage little."

This wise and extremely quotable message resonates with many people. At an early stage in my career, I heard

Buffett speak in person at a human resource executive conference for Fortune 500 companies.

He uttered this phrase at the opening of his presentation and then shared a story about two companies he invested in and their different management styles.

Buffett spoke of the challenges and slower growth rate of the company that overmanaged their business versus the amplified growth of the other organization that hired well and used a more hands-off approach.

He also showed the length of time and due diligence performed for both companies as it related to hiring a leadership team. The hire-well company spent much more time in recruiting and developing the ideal team for their business.

Buffett's message sticks with me today because he provided such a clear and powerful context that every HR executive in the audience could understand and relate to.

And instead of presenting both companies' results side by side on one slide, he first shared the overmanaged company's information, then that of the hire-well organization and then showed the comparison of the two.

The audience of HR professionals knew from his opening line what the results would yield, but his contextualizing the data and results got everyone in the audience nodding and recognizing the importance of his message.

When you look to have an engaging conversation, provide a context that the person you are speaking with can relate to.

Clarity

Clarity is probably the most important component of the Seven Cs and unfortunately one of the most overlooked.

It is difficult to engage your audience if they don't fully understand what you are talking about.

Even more to the point, you cannot connect if your audience cannot clearly hear or understand the words coming out of your mouth.

We often forget that an essential ingredient in engaging content is communication that is clear, easy to understand, easy to digest and easy to listen to.

The last thing you ever want to do in a conversation is confuse the other person.

Keep a keen eye and ear on making sure you are clearly understood when you speak and that your content is easy to comprehend.

Creativity

When content is presented in a truthful, genuine, honest and authentic light, it resonates more with the audience.

Original content tends to incite our senses versus content that's a bit commonplace, tired and unimaginative.

So rather than focusing on how much, how little or what type of "creativity" needs to be deployed to engage an audience, it is more important to deliver, communicate, share and put forward your *own* original thinking.

The audience might not always agree with your point of view, but they will be stimulated by original ideas and thoughts.

In fact, if you look back on some of the most controversial and confrontational conversations you have had in your life, odds are you and your conversational partner might have been on different sides of the spectrum. And while it might not have immediately led to a positive outcome or even brought you closer together, it was probably one heck of an engaging moment.

To be clear: creativity and new ideas don't always find their way into a conversation. However, when they do, creativity can be one of the more powerful elements of the Seven Cs.

Continuity

We hate to be interrupted.

There is nothing worse than when you are fully engaged with informative, brilliant, energizing, meaningful content and something or someone breaks the flow.

We can't stand it if we're in the middle of watching an entertaining program at home and the doorbell rings or someone pops into the room to ask a question. If someone's mobile device goes off at a movie theatre or at a live theatre performance, everyone in attendance feels ill will toward the owner of the device. We even cringe when an interviewer interrupts their subject.

So, it stands to reason that we are completely pissed off if someone interrupts us when we are having an engaging conversation.

This is why continuity and maintaining the flow of content is such an important aspect of engaging your audience.

We enjoy the unbroken flow of absorbing great content because our minds are in the midst of being stimulated and engaged.

Our body actually produces endorphins when we are fully engaged with rich content; thus, a sudden halt literally cuts off the good feelings we are experiencing.

To cater to this desire to maintain continuity, you need to aim to deliver an unbroken and seamless flow when communicating so your message fluidly connects with your audience.

Keep your topics limited and related to each other. If you jump all over the place and bounce from one subject to another, it will be very difficult for your audience to follow.

Keep a continuous, consistent theme throughout and you'll naturally achieve a high level of engagement.

The same applies to one-on-one conversations. Aim to finish one subject of a conversation before moving on to the next.

When a logical break in the flow of the content does take place, try to pick up where you left off. The continuity will bring you right back to the engaging conversation you had before.

Cadence

Think about how a talk show interview has a set format with the host and the guest.

There's a greeting, a check-in, an update, some funny banter, a lead-in to a humorous moment and then some promotion or plug.

Podcast programs have similar formats.

In watching or listening to a conversation as an outsider, we are engaged when there is a familiar structure.

We know what to expect, and that familiarity is comforting and tends to keep us engaged.

When it comes to being an active participant in a conversation, an engaging conversation is more like a dance. The two parties might start out at a different beat; however, as the conversation progresses, a common rhythm is established.

A great conversation has a familiar cadence, and the two parties find a pacing that works together.

Think about two lifelong friends who haven't seen or spoken to one another in a while.

It doesn't take too long for the two friends to "fall into a groove" and be back in the cadence and have the rapport with each other that they had in the past.

We find a rhythm that works well with another and aim to speak at a pace that makes both participants comfortable. Each follow-up conversation with that same individual will likely fall into a similar cadence.

The goal is to try to find that familiar cadence to keep both parties engaged.

Connection

Remember, the goal of a conversation is to create a connection so you can have *more engaging* conversations.

Look for commonalities when you are having a conversation.

Those shared points of interest are often where you find common ground and start to establish a connection.

Combined with the other Seven Cs, your conversations can begin to establish the bond you set out to achieve.

CONNECT, ENGAGE & WIN

As you think about an engaging conversation, whether personal or for business, review your approach ahead of time to see if the Seven Cs *resonate* for the audience you are about to connect to.

Are you going to speak about familiar content within a relatable context?

Even though you are familiar with what you're going to talk about, are you going to communicate your thoughts and message in a clear, easy-to-understand manner?

Will you share content through an authentic lens that demonstrates the creativity within you that is unique to your specific circumstances?

Can you speak with a continuous flow and a familiar cadence that will keep your audience engaged?

Will you find a way to connect your thoughts and ideas, which in turn will establish a connection with whom you are speaking?

The more of the Seven Cs you're able to incorporate as you converse, the more likely you'll achieve an engaging conversation.

3

SOUND CHECK

MARK: *Say something—anything.*
JOANNE *(into the mic): Test—one, two, three…*
MARK: *Anything but that.*
FROM THE 1996 BROADWAY MUSICAL *RENT*

I N 2000, I had the amazing good fortune to be part of a special promotion that centered on the concert tour of the multiple Grammy-winning artist Sting.

One of the perks was that I was able to attend several live performances. I also got to sit in during Sting's rehearsal sessions with the band and the technical team.

In addition to having this awesome opportunity to listen to Sting perform and rehearse, I took away a very important lesson from David Sims, the sound engineer for Sting and his touring band.

David and I met at the tour's first stop in Austin, Texas. He introduced himself to me as a lifelong roadie. David has traveled around the world several times and has worked for almost every major performing artist at one time or another.

At this venue in Austin where Sting was to perform, David brought me to the control panel of the largest sound board I had ever seen.

The next time you are at a live concert, pull your eyes away from the stage to somewhere about three-quarters of the way back on the main level and you'll see the most important piece of equipment for every live music performance.

I used to think that a rehearsal was all about the artist and musicians doing a dry run ahead of the live show. But David shared with me that every stage, arena or stadium requires unique settings on the sound board for each musical instrument and microphone to achieve the optimal quality of sound for that venue. The sound check is a crucial component in ensuring a live performance goes off smoothly with limited problems.

During that first encounter, I learned from David that, more than being a dry run for the musicians, the sound check is about making sure the quality of the listening experience resonates properly across the entire venue to best engage the audience.

Mock Tales

You all know the adage "practice makes perfect."

Musical performers, professional athletes, film, television and stage actors all rehearse and practice ahead of their performances or events.

For weeks on end, Broadway shows rehearse all aspects of the production before the audience files into their seats and the curtain goes up.

Professional speakers rehearse the delivery of their keynote addresses dozens of times ahead of stepping onto the stage and sharing their message.

Preparation ahead of communicating great content increases the likelihood of it being engaging to the audience.

So, if conversations are a form of content and we'd like to have them be more engaging, why aren't we spending more time rehearsing them?

More specifically, why isn't it common practice to do a "sound check" of the content we would share within a conversation to hear how it would resonate with our audience?

It might seem odd to practice what you would say in advance of talking to another individual. Some people might argue that it would be difficult to simulate an authentic conversation ahead of having the actual conversation. But would it be?

For years recruiters and headhunters have recommended and conducted "mock interviews" ahead of an actual job interview. Mock interview sessions provide a candidate with the opportunity to share their story, relate their experiences, connect and convey why they would be a good fit for the position, in a safe environment.

Just as a bartender tries their new concoctions before serving them to patrons, rehearsing what you might say in a conversation provides you with a chance to get a taste of what your words sound like when said aloud.

Career centers at universities work with undergraduate students as they seek opportunities in the workplace to develop and rehearse their own TMAY—Tell Me About Yourself. It's a nice icebreaker and a short, simple way to share with others what you are all about.

Now, by no means am I suggesting that ahead of every conversation you run through all possible scenarios of anything and everything you may talk about.

However, practicing certain components of a conversation that arise most often, like a TMAY, is an effective use of the sound check and of upping the chances of having what you say resonate.

These components that are worth rehearsing alone or in front of other trusted peers I like to refer to as Mock Tales—small *sips* of conversations or *bite-size* stories that are your go-tos when you engage with others.

What you do for a living, where you come from originally, what you do for fun are all common things you might share in a conversation that can be practiced in advance.

There are several ways you can execute a proper sound check. Like a mock interview, you can seek out a close friend, family member or colleague and bounce your Mock Tales off them.

If you're by yourself, rather than speaking in front of a mirror, opt for recording your Mock Tales on your computer or mobile device. If you're an overachiever, you can even video-record yourself. However, make sure to focus on how your message resonates versus how you appear onscreen.

When rehearsing your Mock Tales, be wary of that fine line between knowing how to clearly converse about a specific topic and sounding too rehearsed. Within your sound check sessions, try to speak in a conversational tone and not like you are reading from a script. Ask your trusted peer what resonated with them and if they believe it sounds natural when you share your Mock Tales with them. When you play back your recorded sound check, put yourself in the shoes of someone listening for the very first time.

What will resonate with your audience the most is not *what you say* but *how authentically* you say it.

CONNECT, ENGAGE & WIN

I addressed earlier that many sales professionals and executives are obsessed with overpreparing slide presentations ahead of business meetings.

And I suggested ditching the slide deck and opting to have a conversation instead.

Taking that a step further, try to utilize the prep time by running through a thorough *sound check*.

Before group presentations, have a member of your team role-play a prospect or client. That individual should ask the really tough questions and the team should work on the most common Mock Tales that are applicable for the situation.

Examples of these might be why your company was founded, what problem your product solves, what your team specializes in and what you can expect if you choose to hire us.

In addition, this is the opportunity to work on engaging in a conversation versus sticking to the presentation deck. After the sound check, talk amongst the team and discuss if the session felt more like a presentation or an organic conversation.

The more your responses come off naturally, the more prepared you are to engage in a business conversation.

4

SHOW PREP

———

"We have a really big show tonight."
ED SULLIVAN

IN JANUARY 2007, I attended an annual conference in South Florida at the Boca Raton Resort & Club.

The speaker they had brought in for this event is truly a legend in our time. He has forever changed in-person conferences and has brought motivational speaking to an entirely new level. It was my fourth year in a row at this industry event, but I was particularly excited about this headliner.

Just before the featured speaker's session, I popped out of the conference room to use the lavatory. Upon my rapid return, I mistakenly opened the door adjacent to the door to the main conference room.

They say there are certain things you cannot *unsee*. Things you witness that shock you, surprise you, even cause your jaw to drop. This was one of those moments.

Here I was, racing back to my chair in anticipation of seeing someone I have admired and respected for years, truly excited to be inspired and elevated by an individual who possessed a larger-than-life personality that matches his immensely tall frame. And upon opening the wrong door, I came to see this individual in the featured speakers' prep room, elevating himself to new heights.

Tony Robbins—bouncing on a mini trampoline!

For those who have had the good fortune of being a part of any of Tony Robbins's live events, he brings an energy that is unmatched. There is an electricity in the air and a sense that you're in for a "workout" that will stretch your mind, body and soul into new and uncomfortable growth.

He gets your heart rate up and your body physically ready to jump to help you unleash your hidden superpowers and desire to be great.

To prepare for this, Tony needs to get upbeat himself to help lead and inspire his audiences.

At that time, this trampoline exercise was his pregame preparation ahead of going onstage and connecting with the audience.

Witnessing it in person was something I didn't quite understand then; however, today it is one of my favorite reminders that you need to be in a certain frame of mind to be an effective communicator.

For your personal show prep, you need to draw from within to truly empathize with your audience.

You need to find your own unique trigger to jump-start yourself as you prepare to connect.

To be at your best ahead of every conversation, you need to connect your v.o.i.c.e.

Connect Your V.O.I.C.E.

As a speaker and podcaster, I use this acronym to help me better connect within my conversations. It has become my personal show prep routine, and it can be helpful for you too.

What follows are the elements and actions you can take so you can connect your V.O.I.C.E.

Visualize

In 2015, Jason Day climbed the ranks to become the number-one professional golfer in the world. Each weekend, Jason would be seen near the top of the leaderboard, and the world became quite familiar with his pre-shot routine when he was seen on the course.

The television cameras would focus on Jason's face to capture the former US PGA Championship–winning Australian closing his eyes before he lined up to take a swing. Ahead of every shot, Jason would stand behind the golf ball with his eyes closed and visualize his next set of actions. He would envision himself walking up to the ball, lining up his golf club, taking a deep breath, beginning to take his club back to the position he was most comfortable with and then taking the swing at the ball.

He'd then open his eyes and try to replicate what he envisioned.

This type of visualization is one that I use before going onstage to speak, beginning a podcast program, kicking off a workshop, phoning a business prospect or simply having a conversation.

While I don't close my eyes like Jason does, I do map out a vision of how I'd like the conversation to go. I imagine what I'd like to achieve during this time and, ideally, where I'd like to take things if I'm able to make a connection.

Tapping into this vision of what I'd like to achieve right before engaging with an individual, an audience, a prospect, a client or even a friend can increase the likelihood that I'll make a good connection at the point of contact.

Opportunity

Every conversation is a gift.

It is a chance to connect with others in this world. It is a moment in time where you can listen, learn and grow just by speaking with others.

And yet most people fail to appreciate the value in it.

Unfortunately, many people look at having a conversation with others in a rather self-centered manner. They view it as an opportunity to talk about themselves, their business, their successes, their problems and only what matters to them.

I call this type of communication "Me Speak."

Me Speak can be easily detected by hearing one individual state an excessive number of times the words "I," "me" or "myself."

Other signs of Me Speak can be found with those that are too focused and concerned about making a good first impression. They are possibly obsessed with how they look, dress or appear to others.

Some engaging in Me Speak are fixated on what they have done and what they have created, and they feel the need to show or present what they have without ever asking if the person they are Me Speaking to even wants to see it.

Simply put, a Me Speaker rarely connects with others through a conversation because they're only focused on themselves.

The *O* in connecting your v.o.i.c.e. when engaging in a conversation is appreciating your *opportunity to have a conversation with another*.

Recognize that this opportunity enables you to learn by listening, ask questions that inspire ideas and create a connection that will be rooted in truth, respect and admiration.

Think of it this way. We always appreciate when someone is respectful, kind, considerate and gracious to us, showing us by their words or their actions. This act— even, simply, the attitude we project— is almost always reflected onto others.

By appreciating the moment and preparing to put forth the best and truest versions of ourselves, we increase the likelihood that we will connect with others and establish a strong, productive relationship.

And I believe that if more people knew that simply *appreciating a conversation* would lead to something great happening, we would have many more great conversations and much less Me Speaking.

Identity

Just as every great stage performer gets into character at the onset of a scene, to prepare for a connecting conversation, even after envisioning a connecting moment and being grateful for the opportunity to speak with others, you need to know your role within this conversation and step into it.

This role is your specific identity for this particular moment.

And what identity do I need for this moment?

As part of connecting your V.O.I.C.E., you need to ask yourself exactly this question as part of your show prep.

Are you the "question asker," armed with curiosity and in need of more data to better understand the situation at hand?

Are you your own personal "emcee," about to introduce yourself or someone you know to a new contact or new group of people?

Are you the "problem solver," who needs to fix a situation and has to be timely and effective within the conversation to quickly respond and react?

Are you the "concerned confidant," prepared to listen to and support a mentee, a friend, a prospect or client faced with a dilemma as they vent?

There are numerous roles we need to step into when we enter a conversation. Each circumstance will dictate a different type of role.

Just ahead of a conversation, amidst this pregame ritual of connecting your V.O.I.C.E., you normally are aware of the role you need to play. Ahead of a sales meeting, a one-on-one chat, a team presentation or a networking event, you have a good sense of your identity.

However, there are some instances when conversations spring up suddenly. Just as great actors can improvise and assume the role they need to, you can find your appropriate identity within your communication interaction.

Stepping into the identity just ahead of the conversation can also act as a useful trigger to keep yourself focused.

Your preparedness will position you as an effective conversationalist.

Charisma

Everyone has something unique about their character.

It is this uniqueness that makes us stand apart from others.

Letting it shine through is akin to unleashing one's own special superpower from within.

It turns out that is the hidden gem and fun part about conversations.

We don't just swap words, thoughts and ideas. We mix in our very own sauces and spices that add tremendous flavor to every conversation we have. It is this special recipe that we offer that makes speaking with others not only palatable, but arguably delicious!

Reminding yourself to unleash your personal brand of charisma when you converse with others is an integral part of making your conversations connect.

Don't hold back. Be ready to share who you truly are.

Energy

The last element of your show prep is to infuse some energy and vibrancy into your conversations.

Put simply: no one wants to connect with a dud!

Think of those lackluster, dry, boring, drab classes you had to endure in high school.

Better yet, think of Ben Stein in his role as a high school economics teacher in the movie *Ferris Bueller's Day Off*. Stein's fame-making scene was highlighted by delivering a monotone lecture that lacked even one lick of enthusiasm and put most of his students to sleep.

Nobody wants to listen to, speak or connect with anyone who fails to register a pulse.

We want to hear, feel and enjoy the "spark" of another human being.

Ahead of kicking off a conversation, raise your energy level.

I stress that you do not need to shout from the rooftops or come off like an explosive case of firecrackers to display your energy.

Just be thrilled that you're about to have a conversation.

As you are appreciating this opportunity, show others by embracing the excitement and incredible fortune you have to connect.

And don't forget to tell your face as well . . . put on a smile, and now you're ready to connect your V.O.I.C.E.

CONTRARY TO WHAT most people will tell you, the overall goal of a sales meeting is not to make the sale but rather to make a connection.

This pregame routine is all about getting yourself in the right mindset ahead of your conversation—focusing on forging the connection you need to not only make one sale but set yourself up for many more of them with this specific individual.

The ritual of connecting your v.o.i.c.e. can be used ahead of making a presentation, delivering a keynote address or speaking to a work colleague about a difficult situation.

Engage your show prep skills to ready yourself for any interaction with an individual or group.

This will keep you focused on "how you need to be" versus "what you need to say."

CONNECT, ENGAGE & WIN

Let's demonstrate how you can connect your V.O.I.C.E. by walking through a popular business activity: an initial sales meeting.

V. *Visualize* how you will go about connecting with your target or prospect. This might entail asking questions to learn about the individual, what they do, what their needs are and where they need help. In turn, you might be asked exactly the same questions. You then could visualize sharing some of the ways you could potentially help this target. You could also envision that this will be the first of many subsequent conversations.

O. Be appreciative that you'll get an *opportunity* to learn about this individual's role within their business. Another great thing that will happen is that you will get a chance to better understand this person themself. Regardless of making a sale, this opportunity to connect is what you should be most interested in.

I. In most initial sales meetings, the role of "question asker" is the *identity* you'll take on. You are trying to gather as much information within this conversation as is needed to be helpful to your target

C. "You do you." Don't be afraid to show *charisma* by adding in some of your personality, humor, interests and the things that make you unique. Be prepared to be open when sharing, including in your physical stance.

E. People love to connect to others with high energy. Gauge the individual you're with and try to raise the *energy* level a little above where they are at. Try to rev your engine when asking your questions and learning about your target prospect. It's sometimes tempting to show more excitement when you are talking about your own work or your offering. Keep in mind that in trying to not overpower the prospect, you might come across as not excited about them. Balance your energy and embrace this opportunity to learn about another person. That is where your connection will be strongest and where the conversation will appear to flow the smoothest.

5

SET THE STAGE

---

*"Anything you find yourself holding back,
it's probably what the audience most wants to hear."*

HOWARD STERN

J ASMINE HAD A fever of 102 degrees.

She called me at 10:30 p.m. on the eve of her biggest client's board of directors meeting. As a rising star amongst the partners at Deloitte, she was scheduled to present a proposal to a Fortune 100 company for a multi-year engagement, in what would be her largest sale to date.

Sounding more like the "before" person in a NyQuil advertisement, Jasmine said to me between sniffles, "I need *you* to do the presentation tomorrow morning. I just won't have the strength to deliver it."

Jasmine was one of the youngest partners at Deloitte at that time, and I'd had the great fortune to be working with her team in the months leading up to this meeting. But while I knew the content of the proposal by heart since I'd compiled it for Jasmine, I was not nearly as familiar with the executive team, let alone the members of the board.

After a few nose honks, Jasmine said, "Come over to my apartment building tonight. I'll leave my notes about the executive team and the board with the doorman."

Jasmine was only a few blocks away from me, so I quickly headed over and was greeted by the doorman with a binder stuffed almost to overflowing and bound with a string to keep it contained.

When I opened it up and began sifting through the materials, I wondered if Jasmine had CIA or FBI connections. Enclosed in the binder was handwritten information about each of the meeting's attendees, in more detail than it was likely any of the board members or executives could personally recall about their own lives and careers.

In addition, Jasmine had prepared a detailed, minute-by-minute timeline of every slide within our presentation and the specific questions that would probably be asked, by each board member, for each topic.

It was as if I had the minutes, agenda, script and discussion notes for the entire meeting before it even happened.

Jasmine had effectively set the stage for my delivery of the presentation. All that was missing was makeup and wardrobe, and I was ready to perform.

This level of detail gave me a sense of comfort and confidence. I knew I was more than ready to stand in for Jasmine at the meeting.

WE ALL LOVE a good show.

And if you've had the good fortune of attending a Broadway production, the feeling you experience is truly uplifting.

The setting, the proximity to the stage and the energy in the air is palpable.

Upon arrival, ushers see you to your seats and hand you a program, *Playbill*.

Playbill is a magazine for theatergoers. Each issue features articles focusing on actors, new plays, musicals and special attractions.

For the specific show that you are attending, *Playbill* contains listings, photos and biographies of the cast, authors, composers and production staff. And more importantly, it contains a list of acts, scenes, songs and their performers (for musicals) and a brief description of the setting specific to that show.

While you might not have a clue as to what the show you're getting ready to see is about, or what the music will sound like, or what the actors will say in the upcoming performance, *Playbill* provides a road map of what is to come.

As patrons arrive and start filing into their seats, before the lights dim, you can see everyone skimming right to the list of scenes of the upcoming show. It's quite fascinating. When we are about to be entertained with something we aren't quite familiar with, we like to know what's coming next.

Easy Es

We love that the structure and format of the entire production is handed to us.

This is true for just about every form of entertainment we ingest.

We are shown movie trailers, both in theaters and on television, before we buy a ticket to watch the show.

On late-night talk shows, we see promotions for that evening's upcoming program with a list of who will be on and sometimes even a few clips of prerecorded conversations between the host and the guest. Often, late-night hosts will tell the audience the exact lineup for the entire show at the conclusion of their opening monologue.

Many podcast programs are similar in that they'll provide the actual show notes of the recorded program for listeners to go over ahead of playing the content.

Whether we're a member of the audience or an active participant in the show or in a conversation, we want to know what's going to happen next.

Here is what I usually say to the guest right before we begin to record a podcast interview:

I'm very excited to be here with you today. I've really been looking forward to this. Now before we get started, I wanted to map out for you how this is all going to go.

For starters, you and I are just having a conversation. We're just two people chatting as if we were grabbing a cup of coffee. I am going to introduce you to the audience, and then we'll have a very easygoing chat. And the best part is, we get to talk about you. I'll ask you a series of questions, and we'll go back and forth.

You know that we'll be wrapping up the interview when I ask for you to tell the audience the best ways for them to connect with you or any promotions you'd like to share. Now, is there anything specific you want me to focus on in our conversation?

Breaking this down into its components, here is why I kick things off this way. I call it the "Easy Es."

Enthusiasm. I really *am* excited and appreciative about connecting with new people. It is one of the true joys about having podcast interviews. I want to share that with the guests.

"Ear to Ear." And since I'm enthusiastic about the upcoming conversation, I'm always smiling. A smile shows that I am happy and lets the guest know that they're about to engage in a fun and friendly conversation.

Ease. I also want to help them feel at ease. Some people might be nervous ahead of a recording, and it's important they focus on just having a chat.

Expedition. By mapping out the journey, I am making the guest even more comfortable and letting them know where we'll be heading. Now, it's not a precisely plotted, step-by-step instructional process that we need to follow. It is more that we're at "Point A," we want to get to "Point B" and how we get there is part of the fun.

"End in Sight." I like giving the guest a bit of a heads-up as to when we need to wrap things up. While it's hard to put a time cap on a great conversation, sometimes too much of a good thing isn't so grand.

This "structure setting" at the top of the conversation is a wonderful way to think about how you set the stage to make the beginning of *any* conversation easy.

We often forget that business meetings and sales presentations are a series of conversations.

It is of utmost importance to set the stage at the top of every business meeting.

The *Playbill* for the business meeting is the agenda.

It is what we "come to expect" and "like to know" before we invest our time attending a meeting.

Experienced business leaders and adept managers make it commonplace to provide a clear-cut agenda for a meeting. In fact, many will print out or email the agenda before the meeting begins.

In external meetings with clients, prospects and partners, business professionals will usually set the stage at the onset of a meeting—delivering introductions, timing of the meeting, topics to cover and goals.

Excellent best practices in setting the stage are usually on display at initial meetings, when we first come to meet and engage with new connections. More often than not, though, many managers fall short in setting the stage for subsequent meetings with outside parties. It seems that as we become more familiar and comfortable with outside business associates, we tend to drop certain formalities.

This is even more prevalent within the internal meetings of an organization. Team meetings, group huddles and even one-on-one manager reviews often lack the benefit and structure of good stage-setting.

Setting the stage with a clear and focused agenda isn't just for initial introductions and primary conversations. It provides a structure we are all familiar with that will increase the likelihood of having a productive conversation.

It also demonstrates that we are appreciative of all of the attendees' time by laying out a road map of what is to come. Setting the stage is a mark of respect.

While it isn't necessary to provide introductions at each meeting, covering the Easy Es can only strengthen relationships within the workplace.

It can also provide clarity and timeliness to keep a work conversation on track.

Set the stage, and you'll start to think of your business meetings more like engaging and connecting conversations.

AS FOR MY stand-in performance "playing the role of Jasmine" in the board meeting, the presentation went extremely well—more of a conversation with the board and executive team. And having Jasmine's detailed information and understanding of the players in the room enabled me to direct the conversation on a path that each of the attendees could relate to.

The only conversation that was better than my interaction and subsequent acceptance of our proposal with the board of directors was getting to tell Jasmine on the phone that we won the mandate.

CONNECT, ENGAGE & WIN

Be excited and enthusiastic about the opportunity to have a conversation.

Make everyone involved within the conversation feel comfortable and at ease.

Provide a clear path toward what you plan to talk about.

Give a heads-up as to how you'd like to conclude the conversation.

If you are providing a literal agenda, make it concise. Use one-word descriptors representing the topics that need to be covered (sales, marketing, operations, and so on). Next to each agenda item, list the names of the individuals that will address that specific topic within the meeting. The simpler the agenda is, the more likely the meeting will head down a path toward being a connecting conversation.

6

SHOW UP

_____

"When the red light is on—you show up!"

LARRY KING

A S A YOUNG kid, I dreamed of one day playing basketball in the NBA.

During my teenage years, I was dead set on making this dream a reality.

To prepare myself for future stardom, I used to practice often and try to mimic the moves of the great NBA players of the day: Julius Irving, Magic Johnson, Larry Bird and, most frequently, Michael Jordan.

Not being able to elevate above the rim "like Mike," the best I could do was stick out my tongue and try to imitate how Michael would take a foul shot.

I actually taped several of his games and must have worn out the VCR rewinding and replaying how he set up at the foul line, memorizing the number of times he bounced the ball and his shooting form.

My professional sports dreams came to an end as I topped out at five-foot-eleven with a so-so jump shot, but I carried over some of these "imitation techniques" when I set out to become a professional speaker.

I used to buy VHS tapes and DVDs of some of the legendary inspirational speakers of my time.

Tony Robbins, Les Brown and Zig Ziglar were just a few of the greats that I watched to study how they delivered their message to a live audience.

When it came to hosting my own podcast interview show, I continued with the "to be the best, you need to learn from the best" mantra.

For this, there was one specific individual I wanted to research and study: Larry King.

It is estimated that Larry King interviewed over fifty thousand people in his lifetime. During his six-decade career, King interviewed many of the most famous political leaders, celebrities and sports people of the day. When the final episode of *Larry King Live* aired on CNN in 2010, after twenty-five years, it was the longest-running show hosted by the same person.

While I can't relate to his cigarette smoking on the air or his numerous (eight) marriages, Larry's easy-going attitude on air and inquisitive interview style was something I could completely connect with.

Larry was once asked what the most important thing was that he did before each program. His response: "When the red light is on—you show up!"

Bottoms *Up*

To this point, most of what I've been sharing with you here at the *Speak Easy* has been focused on what you can do *before* you have a conversation.

As any good bartender will tell you, the more prep work you put in before the bar opens, the better you'll be able to serve your guests as they arrive.

Spending time slicing fruit, laying out glass- and stemware, taking stock of inventory and clearing a workspace in advance makes for a smooth, expedient and tasty delivery of your cocktail creations.

If you've thought about your Seven Cs, connected your V.O.I.C.E. and warmed up with the Easy Es, you have done your prep work and are more than ready to stir up a conversation.

To Larry King's comment, it is time to show up as you begin to have a conversation.

I like to think of this term, "show up," in two different but equally important ways.

The first way to interpret show up is by its intended and original definition... to *be present*. Be present, be attentive and be in the moment.

This is what I believe King was referring to when he said "show up," and I completely agree with his thinking behind this very important lesson ahead of having a conversation.

The opportunity to have a conversation is a true gift, and by showing up, you are showing the person you are speaking with that you are focused on them.

You are attentive and intentional in making a connection with them.

You are present to what they have to say.

You physically showed up, and you are also mentally prepared to engage with them.

Larry King wanted to highlight that when that red light turned on and the program was being broadcast live into millions of homes, he wanted to make sure that every viewer felt the attention, energy and focus that he was giving to his guest.

He acted as though his viewers weren't sitting in their living rooms, but right next to the very guest he was interviewing.

He showed up for every episode because he authentically cared about the conversation he was going to have and that the audience would care too.

Building on what King said, I have a second interpretation of his mantra . . . a slight "twist," if you will, and the second way of thinking of the term.

What Do We Mean by Show *Up*?

I'll start off by explaining that when I say the words "show up," I intentionally place the stress on the word "up."

Like in the terms "amp *up*," "fire *up*," "gear *up*" and "game *up*," the word "up" is all about positively and preparedly lifting oneself to another level.

When we "show *up*" in a conversation, we need to be thinking about doing the same.

When we "show *up*," we elevate the relationship from someone you're speaking with to someone you are connecting to.

When we "show *up*," we raise the level of *our* game by lifting up our spirit.

When we "show *up*," we aim high with the goal of improving ourselves simply by having a conversation.

When we "show *up*" in a conversation, we share the best, most elevated versions of ourselves.

How to Show *Up*

How do we show *up* through our conversations? Funny you should ask.

All the previous prep work has been leading to having an authentic, unscripted conversation with purpose.

And that purpose is all about making a connection.

A connection that will bring ideas, thoughts and personal worlds together.

Now I want to be very clear. There is no ideal pairing of words, thoughts and suggestions. There is no utopian road map that brings every conversation to a perfect place. And this section is not going to provide you with the "perfect things to say" with each and every conversation you might encounter.

That is an impossible task (trust me, I've thought about it, researched and tried) because the scope, realm and range of what conversations can cover is infinite.

What this section *will* provide are three helpful techniques we throw around here at the *Speak Easy* that have been used by some of the best interviewers and conversationalists to help you show *up*. They are designed to help you establish a comfortable flow, tap into the beauty of an unscripted conversation and to "speak easy" in the moment.

1. Give It Your A.L.L.: Ask, Listen, Learn

Most longtime talk show hosts and podcast interviewers don't know their guests that well.

In fact, Larry King once shared that even after hosting for thirty years, over 75 percent of the guests he met for the very first time while interviewing them on the program.

That's why the types of questions he asked his guests made it appear to the viewing audience that this meeting was a first encounter. It usually was.

That's not to say that he hadn't done his show prep. He'd know a bit about the interviewee; maybe he even read some of their book (most hosts don't read the book at all). But beyond that, not much background research on each guest.

Larry would *ask* many of the basic questions you'd pose to get to know someone. For example, after his salutations, he'd begin by asking, "Where are you from?" and "How long have you been doing what you're doing?"

He'd *listen* to the response. He'd *learn* something right off the bat. Store the information in his head. And then he'd repeat the process by asking a sequential question based off the guest's response.

He rarely had a preset list of questions he wanted to ask.

He'd let the guest drive the conversation, organically.

As the conversation progressed, he'd often recall one of those "learnings" in helping to pose his next question back to the guest.

King once said, "I'm always engrossed in the guest. I'm always listening to the answer. I'm always learning, so I guess I'm better every day at learning."

Ask. Listen. Learn. When you give it your A.L.L., you begin to create a rhythm to the conversation.

This rhythm and the willingness to "go with the flow" in an unscripted manner creates a trust between the two people speaking.

That trust can enhance the cadence and lead to a more open, honest and deeper conversation that taps into authenticity when you connect.

Show *up* by giving it your A.L.L., and watch your conversations transform into connections.

2. Ask for Permission

It's not only valuable to ask great questions within your conversations, but it's also essential that you ask permission to do so.

As you begin to cover specific topics you'd like to have in your conversation, you want to make sure the person you are speaking to is comfortable having *that* conversation.

Asking for permission demonstrates respect and courtesy, both of which help to establish trust.

This important second theme to help you best show up for your conversations is a very important tactic across many sales and marketing methodologies. Asking for permission is at the center of a growing sales strategy known as permission-based selling (PBS).

PBS is derived from permission-based marketing, a strategy that revolves around consumers opting in to receive promotional offers and announcements from a brand.

By asking for permission to proceed down a line of questioning, the prospect or target opts in to or out of what they'd like to discuss with you.

It is a very helpful framing technique to set boundaries and build a connection within your conversation. This simple act of courtesy inherently shows that the one asking for permission values what is important to the other and cares enough to ask.

Asking for permission demonstrates a level of respect that builds upon the trust being established through giving it your A.L.L.

And it is so easy to do.

Simple transition questions like "Is it okay if I ask you about..." and "May I inquire why..." are great permission-based lead-ins.

In most instances, you're going to hear "yes" when you ask for permission.

Even more importantly, should you hear "no" after requesting permission, you have learned where a boundary is. And being considerate enough to ask before leading a conversation toward a dead end will also save you a lot of time.

In time, your conversation partner might grant you the permission you are seeking once they feel more comfortable with you. Later in your conversation, they could be more willing to address a topic they initially did not grant permission to when you continue to extend the courtesy of asking permission in the first place.

This second technique to help you best show up for your conversations is the easiest one to execute, yet the one people forget the most.

Remember your manners!

Ask for permission, and you'll demonstrate that you are a person worth connecting to.

3. Be You

When you think of showing up for conversations, it would be hard to not bring up an individual who has been showing up for his millions of listeners and fans for over forty years.

Howard Stern, the television and radio personality best known for his nationally syndicated radio program, *The Howard Stern Show*, epitomizes showing up in his approach to interviews.

While Stern was initially recognized for much of his outrageous and risqué topics and material in his early years, over time he has been identified as one of the most authentic, effective and memorable interviewers and conversationalists.

His uncanny ability to get anyone to discuss just about anything has created some of the most entertaining conversations ever recorded.

He captured his meteoric rise across the airwaves in his autobiography *Private Parts*, documenting his journey from local program director to self-proclaimed King of All Media.

One of the most fascinating things that happened in *Private Parts*, which was highlighted in the motion picture of the same name, was when Stern and his first wife, Alison Berns, realized what connected most powerfully with his listening audience during one specific show.

He had been doing numerous funny bits and skits throughout his career. In many of them, he spoke in a silly voice or pretended to be someone he was not. He also invented stories to try to make his topics of conversation a little more entertaining. This would not only happen during his segments on his radio programs, but he'd also carry over some of his act and storytelling into the local advertisements he'd read live on the air.

Here is a snippet from the script of an important scene captured in the movie *Private Parts*:

(Howard ad-libbing as he searches for ad copy.)

HOWARD: WCCC also wants to remind you that our new sponsor Stanley Sport, um, is a great place to go. You know, I got to tell you something. When I was a child, I used to go to Stanley Sport all the time. I loved Stanley Sport. My parents would take me through there, and we just had a great time. And we could walk out with tons of stuff even though my parents didn't make a lot of money.

(Howard pauses and recognizes he's goofed.)

HOWARD: Oh. And, uh, "There's only one Stanley Sports, and the grand opening is this weekend. Mark it on your calendar." The grand opening is this...

(In an honest, apologetic tone, Howard confesses.)

HOWARD: I just realized, uh... that makes no sense what I just said. I just told you I went there as a kid, and now the grand opening... Well, I just... I think I was just caught in a lie. Oh, boy. You know what the truth is? I'm a disc jockey who makes $250 a week, and I just want to do the right thing here on the air. I don't want to get fired, so, uh, I guess I lied to you, but, uh, I'll never let that happen again. You know what I mean? Oh, boy, do I feel stupid.

(Later that day...)

ALISON: Seriously, I heard the show today. I think you're really getting good.

HOWARD: What part did you like in particular?...

ALISON: You know when you did that ad, when you were just being yourself?

HOWARD: That's what you liked?

ALISON: Yeah.

HOWARD: Really?

Howard had identified that what people wanted to connect with was him.

It wasn't a funny voice, a gimmick or an imitation that connected with his listeners; just "being Howard" was what resonated most.

By being himself, he was able to pierce through the airwaves and connect most effectively to his listener.

This then became an integral part of his programming and one of the reasons for his unparalleled success.

What Howard learned was that the most important way to show up was to *be you*.

I believe that at some point in our lives, each and every one of us feels that we need to be like someone else.

It might have to do with our inexperience or lack of familiarity of how to be in a certain circumstance. And that unfamiliarity might be layered with an underlying fear of letting others know that we are inexperienced.

This fear might lead us to behave or communicate in a way that we think would be pleasing to others but might be unnatural or not true to ourselves: imitating others who are more experienced, or saying things in a way we think others would be comfortable with.

Instead of just reading the advertisement as it was written, Howard may have felt that ad-libbing a made-up story about spending his childhood at Stanley Sports would be what people would want to hear. That maybe he could potentially impress the sponsors and his bosses.

He may even have thought that using his silly voice in delivering the ad would make his story even more effective in selling to listeners.

Ahh, sweet irony. Not only was his made-up, inauthentic delivery of the ad spot ineffective, his open and honest confession over the air became one of the first times he truly was himself and connected to his audience.

Howard wasn't the only interviewing great and host to appreciate the power of authenticity.

Media icon and television legend Oprah Winfrey has made authenticity and focus the cornerstone of her style and her brand across all of her businesses.

During her long run as a television host, she was known for her piercing gaze as she interviewed guests.

She believed that she needed to deliver her openness and honesty in a way that was carried through the camera lens, across the airwaves, to and from satellites, through the television sets and into the living rooms to connect to her viewing audience.

Oprah was once quoted as it related to her interviewing style as saying, "What we're all striving for is authenticity, a spirit-to-spirit connection."

She strived to bring out the truest and best version of herself, which would draw out the same great qualities in her guests.

Achieving this "spirit-to-spirit connection" could never happen if Oprah was being inauthentic or was pretending she cared in her conversations.

She lives and breathes this authentic version of herself each and every day.

Oprah Winfrey didn't become one of the most successful business icons in the media industry by faking it!

She earned it by being the best version of herself.

Let Howard Stern's and Oprah Winfrey's lessons be yours. *Be you!*

The preconceived notions of who we think we need to be never match up to who we truly are.

The world wants to connect to *you*... not the person you think you need to be.

When you show *up* and *be you* in a conversation, your connections will treat you as the VIP they *want* to connect to *and* have more conversations with.

I LOOK BACK on those days as a kid practicing at the basketball hoop in my driveway and think how ridiculous I must've looked. Especially with my tongue hanging out of my mouth as I failed to reach the height needed to dunk a basketball and got stuffed by the rim.

The ironic part about the time spent trying to be like Mike was that I developed certain skills and techniques that were distinct to my game.

My unique arms, long for my body frame, helped me create ways to shoot that were difficult for defenders to block—an awkward, gangly style of taking a jump shot that became part of my repertoire.

Not that it was worthy of an NBA salary or a sneaker deal, but it at least made me a respectable contender when sides were being chosen in a local pickup game.

In the realm of public speaking, I was never going to speak or sound like Tony, Les or Zig.

Observing their unique speaking styles helped clarify that I did not communicate or present as they did.

Yet over time I was able to find my own voice, style and delivery that best displays who I am.

CONNECT, ENGAGE & WIN

The message I share with top sales professionals around the globe when it comes to showing up is to aim to be the "host" versus being the "guest" in prospective business conversations.

Every talk show host or podcast interviewer is tasked with asking great questions that the guest answers, which creates an engaging conversation. Your goal should be to do the same—ask great questions as if you were the host—in a business meeting, conversation or presentation.

While both parties in a business conversation are learning about one another in an initial meeting, the one asking the questions is the one driving the conversation.

The more questions you ask, the more you can cater your answers to your target.

When you show *up* in a business conversation, you need to authentically demonstrate that you are appreciative of the time you've been given to converse.

When you show *up*, you need to demonstrate that *the way you are* in this conversation *is how you always will aim to be*.

If you've ever wanted to stand in Oprah Winfrey's, Howard Stern's or Larry King's shoes, you can get your chance every time you're in a sales meeting when you show *up* for a conversation.

Simply remember to give it your A.L.L., ask for permission as you proceed through your meeting and be yourself.

Then watch your audience move from being a potential prospect to a future client.

7

FUN STREET

"The world is filled with negativity. I want people to watch me and think, 'I feel good, and I'm going to make somebody else feel good today.'"

ELLEN DEGENERES

BRENT SAVERS CHECKED his phone and saw an email from one of his longtime clients:

> Brent, I have to connect you to the Dalrymple Group.
> I know that there is something "there there" and that you'll get along with the founder, Sophia.

Initially, Brent thought that this was an odd pairing. He specialized in marketing and rebranding of well-known companies and products, while the Dalrymple Group was a highly exclusive boutique financial advisory firm with little to no public marketing materials.

Brent and Sophia met for lunch.

A few hours later, Brent's longtime client received the following message from Sophia:

> Thank you for connecting me with Brent, I can't remember the last time I had *that* much fun at a business meeting. I'm not exactly sure right now how we can work together, but I want to figure out how we can...

Brent later shared that since he didn't know much about the Dalrymple Group, he didn't feel comfortable "talking shop." He also respected the sensitive and private nature of their work. So instead their entire conversation revolved around who they were and what they liked to do for fun.

The time flew by while the two shared jokes and hilarious experiences. Then they both needed to get back to work.

Sophia's parting words to Brent were "I have no idea what you do, and I haven't been forthcoming to share what we do at Dalrymple, but I'd love to continue speaking and figuring out how we can . . . continue speaking."

Brent and Sophia had just spent some time on "Fun Street."

Fun Street Is Where the People All Meet

One of the reasons we connect through great conversations is that we have fun while having them.

Conversations make us feel good, and we love having fun! That's one of the reasons we don't want a great conversation to come to an end.

Moreover, we are more likely to remember how we *feel* about a conversation than we are to remember the specifics discussed.

Sophia couldn't recall the last time she "had *that* much fun at a business meeting," and she didn't even learn how Brent could help her. Yet she recognized the feeling of a jaunt down Fun Street was worth revisiting and continuing the conversation.

Somehow, though, especially when we are having a business or work conversation, we often forget to inject fun into the mix.

Most are familiar with the saying "All work and no play makes Jack a dull boy." Without time off from work, a person becomes both bored and boring.

Well, that's also true about conversations. Adding in some fun will create a more memorable conversation and will also bring people closer together.

We are used to witnessing fun times when we view engaging conversations from afar.

Broadway musicals or plays with serious subject matter often have a bit of comic relief thrown into the dialogue.

Late-night talk show interviews always include some funny, witty story in the conversation with a featured guest. Some talk shows will even incorporate gags or fun games for the host and guest to play.

You're more likely to remember and recall the fun activity the host and guest experienced together than the specific topic of their conversation.

Trying to make the conversation fun and engaging while still being productive is a true balancing act. But a little effort goes a long way when you're intentional in making your conversations fun and engaging because a trip down Fun Street is worth the cost of admission!

CONNECT, ENGAGE & WIN

Riding down Fun Street is a great tactic to help make your conversations more engaging and increase the odds of how you can connect, engage and win.

The *Thrive LOUD* podcast has a dedicated segment toward the end of each episode that's called "Fun Street." Within this segment, the guest is presented with a set of rapid-fire questions where the answers are all about things that make them feel good about themselves and things they love and truly enjoy.

You can use these suggestions as icebreakers to start conversations or as a way to close meetings on a high note.

"Share something fun." Whether in introductory meetings, weekly team huddles or board meetings, kick-start your conversation by having at least one person share something fun they have planned. Whatever it is, hearing what others like to do establishes a happy, upbeat tone.

"What are your favorite things to eat?" We all have different tastes and attitudes toward food, but we all have to eat. A large sales team of a Fortune 500 company concludes every weekly sales call with one person sharing a recipe of something they love to prepare. This feature became so popular that the company created a special blog section on their corporate website with a new recipe each week.

"Tell us about an activity you wish you did more of." Too often work gets in the way of our getting to do the things we really love. Asking and sharing what activities you love to do helps you to connect. It's fun to learn what people like and even more fun when there's an overlap of interests.

"Talk about an activity you wish you did less of." On the flip side, learning what people don't like doing can also be enjoyable because you can commiserate with each other. Find some shared joy when you learn someone else dislikes doing what you dislike. That's called making "unfun" fun.

"If you could go anywhere in the world . . ." While we may not all love to travel, we all have a favorite place. Learning where that spot on this planet is for each of us is always intriguing. In addition, you'll be amazed at how many people have been to some of your favorite places. It is always fun to share common experiences.

8

LAST CALL

"Good conversation is as stimulating as black coffee, and just as hard to sleep after."

ANNE MORROW LINDBERGH

EIGHT TIMES!
My entire family began counting from the moment that I answered the call.

It has become an inside joke and friendly wager every time I engage in a conversation with Antoine, my friend of many years.

We don't get to see one another that often, and it's always nice to catch up with him.

While our conversations are always fun, informative and entertaining, Antoine tends to go on and on. He is also one of the fastest-speaking humans on the planet, so it is often difficult to get a word in edgewise.

This combination makes it difficult to try to bring the conversation to a close.

Each time I try to end the call and fail to do so, it seems that I emote a similar reaction, displaying my inability to wrap the conversation without being rude: a combination of a headshake of mock frustration and an eye roll of complete disbelief in not being able to say goodbye.

In this instance, it seems the tally reached eight before I finally managed to interrupt Antoine and end the call.

NO MATTER HOW much fun it is to hang out and chat with everyone at the *Speak Easy*, when the bartender hollers "last call," it's time to settle your tab, say your goodbyes and head on home.

Most times it is hard to leave because so many great connections are being made, fueled by great conversations.

I've conducted hundreds of podcast interviews over the years, and it is still incredibly rewarding to hear the following after the recording has stopped: "I gotta tell you. This interview was so much fun that I really didn't want the conversation to end. Thank you for having me on this program. Can we do it again?"

It validates that a connection was made and the guest had a great time.

While we'd all love to continue chatting and connecting in an engaging conversation for hours, it is important to wrap up a conversation in what I like to refer to as "last call."

Remember, the goal of a conversation is to connect... so you can *have more conversations*!

That is how you establish strong, powerful relationships and connections that grow your business and your world.

Therefore, it is critical for the continued growth of a connection that you bring a conversation to a close and set up the next great chat.

Here are some thoughts and steps around helping you wrap up your conversations and continue the momentum to build on your connection.

You Already Set the Stage for Last Call...

If you were able to give a heads-up when you set the stage, you've set an expectation that this magical moment in time would eventually come to an end.

By following through on the expectations you set out at the beginning of the conversation, you have demonstrated that you are accountable for your actions. Wrapping up on time and with respect establishes a sense of trust because you deliver on your promises. Whether it was a set time when you needed to wrap or you've covered all the topics you intended to, you've now created a space where asking for a follow-up conversation is warranted.

"Did We Cover Everything?"

Last call is an ideal opportunity to check and make sure you covered all of the items you had set out to talk about in your conversation.

Conversations can, and often do, head off in unexpected directions.

Last call can act as a checkpoint to possibly redirect the conversation or open the door to set a time to have the next conversation.

Remember the O...

In connecting your v.o.i.c.e., you reminded yourself to appreciate the *opportunity* to have a conversation and the gift that you've been given.

One of the most effective ways to wrap up your conversation is to begin by sharing that appreciation. "I can't thank you enough for taking the time to speak with me today" is probably the most used expression to close talk show and podcast interviews. It also is a spectacular lead-in to one of the last questions you will have during this encounter...

"When Can We Speak Again?"

The last call of one conversation incites the thirst to have another. Before you part ways, satisfy this craving and identify the next and soonest opportunity to meet again to pick up where you left off.

Asking for the opportunity to speak again is your first call to action so your connection and relationship has the opportunity to thrive.

Action Items

If "setting the stage" is the equivalent to a meeting agenda, then "last call" is the next steps or the action items you need to work on ahead of the next business meeting.

These next steps could be as simple as setting up another meeting and inviting others who need to participate in the conversation.

Last call is also an ideal time to address the topics you have yet to cover, which can lead to further learning about one another in a follow-up conversation.

CONNECT, ENGAGE & WIN

There is nothing more gratifying in the sales process than to see a conversation within a meeting begin to establish a genuine connection.

However, many times the conversations within the meeting can run longer than the allocated time, and the meeting must come to an abrupt halt with no clear next steps or action items.

To be clear, in a business setting, the meeting cannot end until you've had last call.

To make certain everyone's needs are served within a meeting, every meeting should have a designated time-keeper. This individual's primary job is not only to make sure the meeting stays on track but also to allocate time for your last call with a few minutes to spare to summarize key action items and immediate next steps.

The importance of summarizing the meeting and what needs to happen next cannot be overstated.

A well-defined last call session with clear "calls to action" can transform an initial conversation into an ongoing business relationship.

In prospective sales conversations, ideally these next steps could entail flushing out the specifics for a proposal to share how you can work together and *help* one another.

Make sure you let everyone in the meeting know who the timekeeper is and that they have permission to interrupt the conversation to let everyone know it's time for last call.

9

OUTRO

"If I had more time,
I would have written a shorter letter."
BLAISE PASCAL

TRYING TO GET across midtown Manhattan during a busy workday is always a nightmare. Sometimes the starting point and destination fail to coordinate with the subway system, and you need to either hail a taxi or use a ride service.

On one rainy Wednesday during the holiday season, Shaun found himself sharing a ride crosstown with Clark.

They met standing outside a building on the east side of New York City. There was one available cab that pulled up to an awning where they were both sheltering from the rain, and they agreed to share the taxi as they both were heading to the west side and knew this was the only option without getting soaked.

Shaun was heading to a client meeting, and Clark was in town from Los Angeles meeting with a few new prospects for his company.

From their initial introduction in the back seat of a yellow cab, it didn't take Shaun very long to make a stupid Superman reference and ask why Clark didn't just fly to his next meeting.

They both smiled and laughed and had a quick back-and-forth conversation. They learned what each one did for a living, a little bit about their family lives and how much they like each other's city.

They had been speaking for no more than two minutes when the taxi came to a complete stop in what seemed to be miles of bumper-to-bumper traffic.

Clark was concerned that he'd miss his next appointment. Shaun asked him where his meeting was. When he shared the company name, Shaun was immediately familiar with the location and knew it was only one block away from a subway station.

"Are you comfortable riding the subway?" Shaun asked Clark.

Most non–New Yorkers have some enhanced fear of the city's subway system. Many believe this has carried over from the 1979 cult movie *The Warriors*, and people are convinced the rail system is filled with city gang members with baseball bats ready to take out anyone that rides the train.

Clark was an exception in that he wanted to take the subway, but he was afraid he'd get lost.

With a few quick directions and the aid of Google Maps, Shaun showed Clark where he could hop out of the cab, catch the train and still make it to his meeting before the taxi would likely even arrive at the next intersection.

Clark thanked Shaun, quickly asked for his cell number in case he got lost and said he'd text him when he got there. Clark hopped out of the taxi and made a dash for the subway entrance.

Not too long after Clark's departure, still in traffic, Shaun's cell phone buzzed with the following message:

Made it through the Underworld thanks to you.
I'm around for 2 more days. Let me buy you a drink to thank you and we can continue our conversation
~ "Man of Steel" ;-)

The next day, that drink turned into dinner.

That dinner turned into a long discussion about Clark's business.

The follow-up conversation a few weeks after dinner turned into a small consulting project for Shaun.

That initial project has since turned into a long-term engagement, which has lasted over four years.

Primarily through a text thread they've named "The Hall of Justice," Clark and Shaun continue to be good friends and use each other as references for work.

Clark and Shaun have both shared the story of that rainy day with others numerous times. Like a "big fish" story, some of the details have been enhanced or exaggerated over time: how hard it was raining, the number of cars piled up in NYC traffic that day, the amount of time Clark had to make his appointment on time or how quickly the subway train traveled.

Yet one part of the story never varies, and it is as true today as it was then: how long they were inside that taxi together... *no more than two minutes.*

If there is one thing I've learned as a conversation- alist, it's that there is no minimum time requirement for making a connection between two people having a conversation.

Due to unique circumstances, Clark and Shaun didn't have much time to get to know each other, build trust and learn how they could help one another. And yet, in a New York minute, they shared a taxi, helped each other out, talked about their professional and personal lives and provided contact information to one another.

Some people believe that a certain amount of time is needed when you have a conversation to feel "comfortable enough" to establish a connection.

I have a different belief.

B5G

In late 2015, I set out to create a new podcast program. At that time, I compiled a series of notes and thoughts around my vision for the show, its format and the specific themes each episode would cover: "Each episode should be short and not too drawn out. The goal for each interview is to uncover the brilliance of the guest and have them share lessons and tactics the listeners could deploy to elevate their own lives."

Within those notes I also found this comment around how I would close out each show: "use a consistent 'outro' for every episode ... maybe 'B5G'?"

B5G is short for "Be brief, be bright, be gone."

It's an expression I heard years ago at an awards ceremony where the recipient being honored stated in his acceptance speech, "Well, I don't want to be up here longer than I need to, so I will be brief, bright and out of here before you know it."

I thought it was quite brilliant. Shortly after, I adapted the phrase, and I thought that it would be a fun line to say at the end of each show.

Over many years and thousands of interviews, my B5G has been the last six words uttered at the conclusion of every podcast episode I have produced as a host. I have also learned that "Be brief, be bright, be gone" is way more than just a cheeky sign off.

I believe that B5G is one of the biggest takeaways and one of the best reminders to help you *Speak Easy* so you can connect, engage and win with every conversation.

CONNECT, ENGAGE & WIN

Be Brief

We live in very busy times, and we have a lot of things to do every day. Time is one of the most valued resources we have. We don't ever really want to waste it.

Understanding the importance of brevity in this fast-paced world is about appreciating the time we have with others.

Recognize that it is truly a privilege to make the time to sit down and have a great conversation with another busy human being.

Make the most of the time you have and be respectful of it by optimizing and being "straight and to the point" within your conversations.

Be Bright

Within the limited time we get to connect to others, we *need* to share our brilliance and our genius.

When we share our genius with others, we are not only adding value and meaning to a conversation, we are also injecting our brilliance into the world.

One conversation can be the starting point of one brilliant idea that changes our lives for the better.

Let your ideas flow out when you connect in a conversation. It could lead to a change we *all* need in the world.

Be Gone

If your first instinct was to think that this is the "mic drop" moment of your conversation, you wouldn't be the first.

But "be gone" is all about moving onward and upward.

Use the learnings and connections you obtained within your conversation as the starting point to elevate your relationship, your business and your life to the next level.

The connection made through a great conversation is a "win" for everyone involved in the conversation *and* everyone connected as well. Because when we move onward and upward, we *thrive*.

In no more than two minutes, Clark and Shaun had a short conversation that led to a long-lasting relationship in business and in friendship. Whether they intended to or not, they engaged in B5G.

Sometimes we carry the notion that we need to extend a conversation to get the most value out of it. Clark and Shaun didn't have that time and were both the better for it.

I think the adage "less is more" rings true more often than not.

If we cut to the chase and drive straight to clearly identifying how we can *help each other*—we'll see more efficient and productive conversations and stronger connections.

B5G enables you to use brevity to establish longevity. You can schedule shorter calls and meetings. You can write shorter emails with more impact.

B5G can be the overarching goal for your conversations, and you'll look forward to having more of them over a longer period of time.

THE *SPEAK EASY* SECRET MENU

B ECAUSE YOU'VE BEEN *such an attentive patron and have been taking the time to learn and sample from our main selection, I wanted to offer you something you won't find on the regular menu.*

At this Speak Easy *we have a special bar cart reserved for our select customers—a reserve selection that I'm sure you will enjoy.*

And since this is your first visit, I will present our bar cart offering to you as a tasting menu.

I like to call it our "conversational flights."

Each of these conversations has its own unique flavor.

Some of them are age-old favorites, and others are new varietals that have recently come onto the scene.

Each flight has a tip or trick, suggested by our in-house mixologist, on how to best prepare, pour or partake with each conversation.

Let me present each one of them to you, and you can see how you might put these conversations to good use in your own time.

SPEAK EASY WARNING

These conversations are mostly those you may encounter within your work or business environment. Many of the ingredients can be mixed for personal use as well, but please use discretion when doing so.

Since this is a "sample size," you will only be presented with a few select varietals that have been deemed the favorites of our *Speak Easy* patrons.

The Icebreaker

Something that serves to relieve inhibitions or tension between people or start a conversation.

Ingredients
3 ounces of intentionality
2 boosts of energy
1 shot of gumption
a dash of nerve
and garnish with a welcoming smile

Goes Great With
Networking events, initial encounters, first day on the job, kick-starting a conversation with someone new, rinsing out an "uncomfortable silence."

Mixologist Tips & Tricks
The anticipation right before starting an initial conversation always feels uncomfortable.

That feeling almost always arises because you are not sure exactly what to talk about going into meeting someone for the first time.

It can be awkward.

Now while you can always just start a conversation by introducing yourself with your name, the company you work for or maybe even what you do . . . no one, including yourself, ever really wants to start a conversation off that way. It's boring, bland and rarely memorable.

At this *Speak Easy*, we believe our Icebreaker is a fan favorite because it makes a strong impact right from the start.

Think of something that you personally like, something that is one of your favorite activities, and introduce yourself with it.

For example, "My name is Janine and I love going to live concerts."

Upon hearing this, the immediate reaction will most likely be "What kind of music do you listen to?"

Or "Who have you recently seen perform?"

Ice broken.

Oh, and here's the bonus: you get to start talking about something you love to talk about.

You'll eventually get to the "who you are" and "who you work for" as you chat ... but this Icebreaker gets right to the heart of what *you* are about.

This tactic will also increase the likelihood of getting the person you are speaking with to open up and do the same.

If you're so willing and want to add an extra shot of gumption, share what you'd like *and* what your superpower is.

"Hi, I'm Veda. I love being outdoors and am in love with kite surfing."

"Hey there, my name is Chris. I love sushi, and I am passionate about teaching children to read."

We love to hear someone's purpose. And when they open with it, we want to learn more *and* want to engage with that individual immediately.

Chris's Icebreaker was one shared directly with me once, and I not only learned he's a reading specialist for elementary school kids across a large school district, I learned later, over a sushi dinner, that he specializes in working with children with autism and was writing a book about it.

Instructions

Embrace the adventure of meeting new people.

Raise your energy level to channel that nervous energy into excitement.

Be warm and welcoming.

Open with what matters most to you.

And don't forget to smile.

The 800-Pound Gorilla (a.k.a. the Uncomfortable Conversation)

A problem or difficult issue that is obvious but is ignored for the convenience or comfort of those involved.

Ingredients
3 ounces of tension
1 shot of lump in your throat
a sprinkle of butterflies
pair with a 4-cup chaser of deal with it

Goes Great With
Awkward moments, uncomfortable silences, difficult employer-employee working situations, looming problems that everyone is afraid to confront.

Mixologist Tips & Tricks
Throughout our lives and working careers we are confronted with situations and dilemmas that, in the moment, appear to be bigger than anything we've ever experienced. When those moments present themselves, most of us are afraid to talk about them.

There is a level of human discomfort that seeps through our pores and makes everyone involved with the situation feel uneasy.

In our personal lives, we'll choose to speak about "anything but" this pressing situation.

In the workplace, we'll often opt to dance around a certain topic, as if we're walking on eggshells, rather than have to deal with the big megillah that needs to be addressed.

In this spirit of what this conversation flight is all about...let's cut to the chase!

The 800-Pound Gorilla looks more intimidating than it really is.

I liken it to the initial reaction you have when your server brings you over one of those massive blue-colored "hurricane" cocktails that are meant for multiple people and are often served in an enormous martini-glass-shaped bowl.

The most common initial reaction people have to this monster's appearance is "There is no way I can handle that."

While the first sip might be hard to swallow, the rest goes down surprisingly easy.

The same is true for the uncomfortable conversation.

When you are presented with this looming matter in life or at work, address it immediately. Failure to do so will only make it appear larger than it really is and distract everyone involved from being able to focus on anything else until it is discussed.

The lump in your throat, butterflies and tension are just garnishes that come with the Gorilla and are truly unnecessary.

Many of our patrons have suggested we rename this drink menu item the 8-Ounce Monkey.

But that might cause people to overlook something that we feel you need to tackle right away.

Instructions

Simply grab that "deal with it" chaser.

Take down the 800-Pound Gorilla as soon as you arrive.

Before you know it, this might become your favorite type of conversation.

The Cash Bar
(a.k.a. the Conversation about Money)

The conversation focused on the price, value and amount of money that is required, perceived as needed or possessed by those involved, or that is being considered for the situation at hand.

Ingredients

3 cups of value

1 ounce of judgment

a splash of discomfort

a pinch of shame and a sense of worth

Goes Great With

Starting a new job, asking for a raise, sharing the value for services required, planning for the future, speaking with family and friends.

Mixologist Tips & Tricks

There is no other conversational flight on the menu that piques more curiosity than the Cash Bar.

Most of the patrons have a very difficult time ordering this item.

Which begs the question: why is it so difficult to talk about money?

There are many reasons, starting with the fact that "the money talk" is not just about dollars and cents, bank balances, price tags, credit card or student debt.

At its core, how we view money is about values, and how those values motivate our behavior.

In a conversation with *Today* about the ways in which financial conversations can cause discomfort, John P. Vincent, a psychology professor at the University of Houston, said, "Discomfort with money talk stems from fear of judgment. For those with few resources, they fear being looked down upon. People may think they are lazy, stupid or a poor money manager. For those with lots of resources, they fear being exploited. People will not like them because of who they are, but for what they have."

This also carries over into the professional world during sales pitches or presentations where there is often an awkwardness in sharing the price of a product, service or offering. The fear of judgment Dr. Vincent outlines is most frequently unleashed when entrepreneurs and solo-preneurs need to share what their services cost.

When this discussion is required, these individuals can be overwhelmed with an uncertainty about their self-worth.

"Does my small business really command the price I'm sharing?"

"If they say no to my price, are they saying I'm not worth it?"

We used to call this conversational flight "the brain freeze" since, for some, having the conversation about money was too overwhelming and almost paralyzing.

I have two key tips on how you can best have the money talk.

1. Lead with your value

While each of us has our own value system, if we see value in something, we will exchange money for it. Therefore, you need to first present *your* value.

If it's to determine how much your salary or raise should be, you need to demonstrate the value you've provided in the past and will continue to provide in the future.

Whatever uncomfortable feeling you have ahead of asking for that raise or for what you believe you should be paid, you can justify your asks when you share with your employers the value you bring to the table.

If you are pricing your own services or offerings, your prospective client *also* needs to see the value you will provide them. If they don't see the value and don't care to pay the price you've presented, then either you haven't presented it clearly or they're not the ideal client for you.

2. Move through fear into courage

The second way to address the conversation about money is to move through your fear of judgment into a place of courage.

Rather than dwelling in the discomfort and fear of how you will be judged by your peers, family, friends and loved ones, flip that fear on its head. Don't stress about being judged; get excited about the opportunity to be appreciated!

Embrace the positive feeling they will perceive in you when they get to see your true worth and value.

Instructions

Start by pouring in your value.

Professional mixologists have been known to make the Cash Bar with value straight up.

However, if you feel you'll always have a little bit of discomfort, shame and judgment, counteract the bitter taste of these uncomfortable additives by adding an extra dose of your worth.

(When you bring that combination to the table, your audience won't be focused on how much it costs; rather they will savor the value they get to taste.)

Honesty... Straight Up
(a.k.a. the Truth Serum)

Nothing but the truth.

Ingredients
1 ounce of flat-out honesty
(Quantities may be increased and should be consistent and persistent throughout.)

Goes Great With
Every conversation you ever have.

Mixologist Tips & Tricks
When it comes down to it, honesty is the key ingredient to every connecting conversation.

It is the linchpin that holds a connection together.

If a conversation lacks honesty, we can usually sense it. Most of us have bullshit detectors that are highly effective. We can smell when someone is lying or being disingenuous from a mile away.

Without honesty, your entire conversation is a flat-out lie that most people won't want to partake in.

Be straight-up truthful and make sure to also be overtly grateful and appreciative at the conclusion of every conversation.

Instructions
Communicate with straight-up honesty every single time.

The Boom Boom Zoom Room
(a.k.a. the Virtual Conversation)

Conversations can take place physically face-to-face, or they can be mediated in some way by technology such as a phone or video-communication services.

Ingredients

4 ounces of honesty
2 double shots of extra attention
2 shots of energy
1 hint of a smile
1 swizzle of gratitude

Goes Great With

Phone calls, virtual team meetings, one-on-one chats, webinars, remote-office work sessions and training, virtual cocktails.

Mixologist Tips & Tricks

How can we be so connected yet feel so far apart?

The advancement of technology in how we communicate continues to bring us together in ways we never could have imagined.

We continue to create more and more devices for us to stay connected to one another.

Telephones evolved to mobile phones...

Audio speaker phones morphed into video conferencing...

Mobile technology put minicomputers into our hands...

Mobile phones enabled us to make video calls...

Video conferencing became accessible on our desktops... and then on our mobile devices...

We now have more ways to see and hear one another than ever before without being in the same city, state or country, let alone the same room.

Yet with all these incredible advances in technology designed to connect us, many have argued that we are becoming more disconnected than ever.

Sure, we can have a virtual conversation on our computers and our smartphones, but we're not truly connecting as we could and would if we were face-to-face.

So, what's missing?

Aside from not being in the same room with the person you're having a conversation, the two key elements of a connecting conversation missing from a virtual conversation are energy and attention.

When Oprah shows up for every interview with her piercing authenticity, she needs to elevate her energy level to connect to her viewing audience.

To connect via a virtual conversation, you must also bring the appropriate energy.

Staring at your computer screen through your virtual camera can be draining.

You and the audience you're connecting to within a Zoom "room" are in different locations and you're not all feeling the same vibe.

Your Zoom room needs a little "boom boom."

To achieve this energy pick-me-up, I recommend literally *picking yourself up*.

I often conduct my virtual presentations and conferences at a standing desk.

It enables me to move my hands as I speak and be on my toes. It's as if I'm onstage and performing when I present virtually.

If you're able to create that setup in your office, give it a try.

Otherwise, if you're stuck sitting in your chair in front of your computer, sit up real tall and lean in to the camera as if you're trying to move closer to your intended target.

Bring that energy.

The other key element that needs to be added to your virtual conversations is focused attention.

When we are having a face-to-face conversation with someone, we don't have multiple computer screens and applications open in front of us.

Usually, the only screen we have handy is a mobile phone. Staring at that screen while having an in-person conversation is bad form and unlikely to lead to a connected relationship.

According to an analysis prepared by the Windows division within the 2020 annual report released by Microsoft, the average person has upwards of eight applications open on their desktop while they are having a virtual meeting.

And that doesn't include the emails, message alerts and reminders that pop up while we're having a conversation.

As the Boom Boom Zoom Room recipe states, you need two double shots of extra attention.

What's the best way to create this environment? To start, shut down your other applications when you're having a virtual conversation.

Note also that when we are many miles away, our "BS radar" can be a bit temperamental, especially with all the other digital interference that is present on a virtual call. This is why our team of mixologists suggests adding quite a bit of honesty and would like to remind you to throw in a thank-you to complete a virtual conversation.

Most of your in-person conversations conclude with a handshake, bow or fist-bump. Communicate your gratitude to your virtual attendees as your sign off to conclude your session.

Incorporating these steps will give more *boom boom* to your virtual conversations.

Instructions

Start with honesty.

Combine the energy and the extra attention that is required.

Top it off with gratitude and throw in a smile to boot.

The Helping Hand (a.k.a. the Service Plug)

Conversations that lead toward promoting one's services.

Ingredients
3 ounces of sincerity
2 shots of kindness
1 large offering of help

Goes Great With
Sales presentations, meet and greets.

Mixologist Tips & Tricks
The Helping Hand was one of those happy accidents created here at the *Speak Easy*.

One of our mixologists was fiddling around with some of the key ingredients in how you ask for permission and posed a good question: since so many conversations amongst the patrons lead to talking about the services they offer, what would be a more tasteful and flavorful way to talk about plugging one's services?

You'll remember that a conversation can establish or grow a personal connection.

Within an authentic, unscripted conversation lies an opportunity for those involved in the conversation to offer help to one another.

That offer of help between connected parties can be viewed as a promotional plug for one's services.

Help is the connection currency.

The output and payoff of a great conversation is establishing how you can help one another. The Helping Hand provides the details and follow-up steps on how those having a great conversation can access help when they need it once the conversation is over.

The real challenge within every conversation is knowing *when* and *how* to tactfully, and playfully, share how you can help one another without seeming forced or coming across as salesy, disingenuous or cheesy.

But when, within a conversation, is the best time to indicate how you can help?

In keeping with the *Speak Easy* run of show flow, the plug section of most interview programming is covered later in the show.

This is not to say you couldn't provide a plug early on within the conversation. However, you cannot offer a Helping Hand until you have been granted permission to do so.

This is why you rarely hear a *service plug* at the beginning of a conversation.

You need to earn the respect and trust that would warrant someone being willing to ask for your help or accept it when offered.

Typically, the Helping Hand is also a great starting point for your next conversation. In fact, it's also known as the service plug because it could very well be a chance to talk about your helpful services the next time you connect.

How you offer a Helping Hand is crucial, and I think it is very important to note the distinction between "selling your services" and "offering your help."

If you approach a conversation with a goal of selling something, odds are you're not going to have a great conversation.

When you approach a conversation with the goal of establishing a connection, you are putting forth your most authentic and best version of yourself, and you're presenting the type of person we want to have help us when we need it.

And what happens next is very straightforward: the person you are speaking with asks you for help directly, or you ask them nicely if it is okay for you to share with them how you can help.

Try not to overthink this. There is an almost natural progression to the conversation and a desire to keep the momentum and the connection.

By this point in the conversation, you've most likely navigated to this logical conclusion. It's the ideal time to share how you can help.

Here are a few segues that could work as ways of asking for permission:

- "Would it be okay with you if I shared how I could help you out?"

- "I'd love to be able to dive into this further—could we set a follow-up time so I can share more details about how we could help each other?"

- "Would you like to hear more about what I do that might help?"

If you ask any of these questions and are met with a "no," you've been pitching and not connecting.

We will always consider help from someone we've connected with through great conversation.

Instructions

Begin with the recommended amount of sincerity and kindness to warm up, but soon you should feel free to add as much as you'd like. (You can never have enough of either one!)

Show and share ample amounts of help—this will expedite your connection.

Never serve with cheese! Be genuine, real and honest.

The I'll Have Another
(a.k.a. the Follow-Up Conversation)

To carry on with, to persevere with, to keep up on, to continue with a previous discussion.

Ingredients
3 cups of picking up where we left off
2 ounces of appreciation
1 shot of gratitude
1 quick pour of a recap
a pinch of pleasantries
and garnish with a familiar smile

Goes Great With
Enjoy after every initial conversation, sales demonstration, first interview.

Mixologist Tips & Tricks
At the *Speak Easy* we have seen many customers return to reconnect with familiar faces.

As you've already learned, one of the goals of having a conversation is to be able to have more of them.

When people reengage, they're looking to recapture that great flavor they all enjoyed the last time they spoke.

And while often it can be very natural to pick up right where you left off, sometimes circumstances, the length of time in between conversations or the new environment might make it challenging to recapture the magical connection that was established previously.

When most patrons look at the special bar cart menu and see the I'll Have Another, they think it's having more of the previous conversational flight they ordered.

Here's our little *Speak Easy* secret . . . I'll Have Another is more like a palate cleanser.

The follow-up conversation is one of the most common action items set up after an initial conversation. Odds are that that conversation needed to come to an end because more information needed to be gathered, other individuals may have been needed for the conversation to continue or more time was required to better understand how the parties involved can help one another. Yet because of the time delay between the original and the follow-up conversations, it is unrealistic, unnatural and arguably weird to literally just pick right back up wherever and whenever you last ended.

I'll Have Another was added to our menu to rinse out any conversational flights you've just taken part in, reset the environment to get you back to where you were before and restart the connection you achieved the last time you had a conversation with this individual or group of individuals.

Here's how you prepare the ingredients for a smooth transition to help you reconnect within your follow-up conversation.

Instructions

Begin with the familiar pleasantries and greetings as you first reengage with all attendees. Keep in mind that there might be new additions to this follow-up conversation, so making introductions is very important.

Whether this follow-up conversation is the first of its kind or it's one of numerous that have taken place in an ongoing relationship, never forget to display your gratitude and appreciation for taking the time to have *this* conversation.

Offer a quick recap to remind everyone of where you previously left off and what has transpired since you last spoke.

Then ask another person in the conversation to confirm the summary they heard and add any information they have.

Make sure that everyone is on the same page as to where the last conversation left off.

Confirm what everyone would like to accomplish during *this* follow-up conversation. (This structure and direction keep the conversation on track and build on the strength of the connection achieved in previous conversations.)

Lastly, don't forget to flash those pearly whites throughout your follow-up encounter. (That warm, familiar smile can add comfort and increase the likelihood of maintaining the connection you've established.)

CONNECT, ENGAGE & WIN

I truly hope that you enjoyed the conversational flights featured on our special bar cart menu.

When followed correctly, our mixologists' tips and tricks can help make each conversation quite alluring, potent and effective in forging the connections you desire.

There are many more types of conversation concoctions that exist—too many to list. However, I hope that even amongst this small sampling of varietals, you will be able to apply some of my suggestions to the conversations you encounter in your business and in your life.

Even though we labeled this a "*secret* menu," I urge you to share these recipes with those on your teams and within your organizations.

In fact, engage in a conversation with them to discuss how these conversational flights might mix into your interactions with your prospects, targets and clients.

And make sure to let them know where they can pick up their own copy of this book—and give it a great review, I hope!

Cheers to you, and thanks for stopping by the *Speak Easy*.

ACKNOWLEDGMENTS

CREATING *SPEAK EASY* was by no means an easy task. Its mere existence would not be possible without the help of so many people across the many different worlds within my universe.

There are too many individuals to thank specifically within this section. Those that I fail to mention, I will make certain to engage with directly in a conversation in the very near future to thank personally.

However, there are a few individuals I need to "raise a glass to" and address their specific contribution in helping me with this project, as well as those most precious and dear to me in my life.

The entire team at Page Two. Trena White, Jesse Finkelstein, Peter Cocking, Taysia Louie, Chris Brandt, Rachel Ironstone and the *ever-so-humble* Adrineh Der-Boghossian. I am forever grateful to you for keeping me on track.

A special thank you to my *editorial mixologist* and *B5G-sister-from-another-mister*, Amanda Lewis. You constantly inspired me and forever reminded me that I'm at my best and do my best writing when I'm having fun.

My clients. Working with you and witnessing your organizations master how to connect has helped me see how engaging conversations grow connections and help them thrive. While you often share how much I inspire you, it is your work and your success that truly inspire me.

My simply awesome speakers mastermind group. Sylvie, Phil, Jill, Bruce, Melanie, Drew, Tami and Ron. Your own careers, lives and successes inspire me every day. Your kindness and brutal honesty keep me focused. I appreciate your constant reminders to unleash my superpowers unto others, along with my smile. Thank you for always elevating me when I need a boost.

My fellow podcasting brothers and sisters. There's a tremendous amount of people doing the world an invaluable service by helping others to connect with their voice through engaging conversations via their podcast programs. I applaud you all for living and breathing the essence of *Speak Easy* every day. It would be unjust if I didn't give the proper kudos to Doug, J.J., Strick, Steve-O, Anna and Christopher for helping me embrace and thrive within this medium.

An enormous debt of gratitude is owed to the *Thrive LOUD* community, comprised of the hundreds of inspiring and uplifting guests on the podcast programs, the dozens of interns that have helped produce this program throughout the years and the millions of listeners that have listened to, learned from and connected with engaging conversations. Thank you all for being part of something that creates connection and value to so many each day.

To all my friends. I cherish every connecting conversation we have ever had and eagerly look forward to having more of them in the future.

To my family. Mom and Dad, I am forever grateful; none of the incredible moments in my life happen without you two. Herb and Fanny, thank you for always being there. My two sisters and brothers-in-law, thank you for always making sure that laughter is injected into every conversation we have.

To Alec and Toby. You continue to be the inspiration of my life, and being your father is *still* the best gig on Earth.

To my wife, Janet. I love you always, and I am forever grateful to spend my life with you.

NOTES

Chapter 1: Conversations Matter

Boom! Dialogue Limited. "New Survey Reveals Average Brit Has 27 Conversations Every Day." Courage Beer press release. August 26, 2010. newswiretoday.com/news/76151/New-Survey-Reveals-Average-Brit-Has-27-Conversations-Every-Day.

Cambridge Dictionary. online. s.v. "conversation," dictionary.cambridge .org/dictionary/english/conversation.

Edison Research and Triton Digital. *The Infinite Dial 2020.* Edison Research online. edisonresearch.com/the-infinite-dial-2020/.

Mastroianni, Adam M., Daniel T. Gilbert, Gus Cooney, and Timothy D. Wilson. "Do Conversations End When People Want Them To?" *Proceedings of the National Academy of Sciences*, 118, no. 10 (March 2021): e2011809118. doi.org/10.1073/pnas.2011809118.

Nielsen Podcast Listener Buying Power Database. "Podcast Content Is Growing Audience Engagement." The Nielsen Company. February 26, 2020. nielsen.com/us/en/insights/article/2020/podcast-content-is-growing-audio-engagement.

Turkle, Sherry. *Reclaiming Conversation: The Power of Talk in a Digital Age.* Toronto: Penguin, 2016.

Chapter 6: Show Up

Lunden, Jeff. "Veteran Broadcaster Larry King Dies at 87." NPR. January 23, 2001. mynspr.org/2021-01-23/veteran-broadcaster-larry-king-dies-at-87.

Marin, Rick. "Howard Stern: The *Rolling Stone* Interview." *Rolling Stone*. February 10, 1994. rollingstone.com/music/music-news/howard-stern-the-rolling-stone-interview-60411.

Stern, Howard. *Private Parts*. New York: Simon & Schuster, 1993.

Thomas, Betty, dir. *Private Parts*. Screenplay by Len Blum and Michael Kalesniko. Los Angeles, CA: Paramount Pictures, 1997.

Bar Cart Bonus: The *Speak Easy* Secret Menu

Callahan, Chrissy. "Talking about Money Doesn't Have to Make Us Cringe. Here's How to Make It Easier." *Today*. August 31, 2020. today.com/tmrw/talking-about-money-doesn-t-have-make-us-cringe-here-t187105.

Microsoft Corporation. "Annual Report 2020." 2020. microsoft.com/investor/reports/ar20/download-center/.

ABOUT THE AUTHOR

LOU DIAMOND IS a highly sought-after speaker, connector, leadership and performance mentor and podcaster. Author of the international best seller *Master the Art of Connecting* and CEO of Thrive, Lou has made it his life's work to help businesses, leaders and brands thrive through the power of connecting.

His innovative connecting tactics have helped hundreds of companies across the globe explode their sales, retain their clients and build a thriving culture.

Lou's boundless energy and motivation have inspired audiences to feel they can conquer the world and make tons of great new connections doing it.

Connect with Lou and more of his work at ThriveLouD.com and LouDiamond.net.

share with others that I was put on this planet to with the most amazing businesses, leaders and brands help them thrive through the power of connecting.

Whether assisting sales teams to better connect to their targets, marketers to better connect their message or leaders to better connect to their people, I've been following my passion and living my purpose through the work I do at my company, Thrive.

As you've learned, all connections begin with a conversation. Since you've taken the time to visit this *Speak Easy*, I would love to have a conversation with you. Connect with @ThriveLOUD on Instagram, Twitter, LinkedIn and Facebook.

To see the work we do at Thrive or to listen to episodes of the *Thrive LOUD* podcast, go to ThriveLouD.com.

If you'd like to learn about having me speak at your company, organization or event, reach out to me at speaking@thriveloud.com, and we can set up a time to have a conversation.

WORD OF MOUTH

It's been over a hundred years since we had to keep a low profile and not let folks know where to find our *Speak Easy*. If you enjoyed what we served up here, we are more than okay with you telling others about it now—in fact, we hope you will. Please scan this code and write a review.

Speak Easy is also available in electronic and audio formats. Please visit SpeakEasyBook.com to access all versions.